Understanding Rese ucation

Understanding Research in Education

K. LOVELL

and

K. S. LAWSON

University of London Press Ltd

SBN 340 09616 0 Board
SBN 340 11822 9 Unibook

University of London Press Ltd
St Paul's House, Warwick Lane, London EC4

Printed and bound in Great Britain by
Neill & Co. Ltd, Edinburgh

Contents

Preface vii

1. The acquisition of knowledge and the aims of research 1

2. Problems and theory in different areas of research 14

3. Descriptive research 29

4. Experimental research 49

5. Instruments of research 1: introduction and tests 64

6. Instruments of research 2: self-report techniques 85

7. Instruments of research 3: observational techniques 108

8. Some statistical concepts related to research 124

9. Examples of research in education 132

Further reading 147

Bibliography 148

Index 153

Preface

For some time we have given a course of lectures to our students on research methods in education. These methods relate mainly to problems connected with children and their learning. Our students' response has been such that we have been encouraged to write down the substance of these lectures in an abbreviated form and without any serious treatment of statistics, for a larger audience. The book does not, of course, deal with research in the administration, history or philosophy of education, although an example of research which provides data on which administrative action could be taken is given in chapter 9. Neither does it deal with the important topic of research in the field of curriculum development *per se*.

Our hope in writing this book is twofold: first, to enable students and teachers to have a better understanding of some of the research methods used in education and of the rationale which underpins them—this includes giving readers an appreciation of a few of the difficulties involved; second, to enable students and teachers to look more critically at research and so put them in a position where they are better able to judge the strengths and weaknesses of a given piece of research work. It is hoped, too, that the role of theory in advancing knowledge has been put into proper perspective. Much of the book should also be of value to undergraduates in the social sciences.

The book was not written with the intention of training research workers in education, although it may well help them to reflect upon their assumptions and methodology. It is expected that readers will be familiar with the terms 'arithmetic mean', 'standard deviation' and 'correlation coefficient', since this book does not deal to any extent with statistics in educational research or experimental design *per se*. There are already many excellent books which deal with these topics.

Finally, readers will appreciate that the book deals with methods that have been devised for use with subject matter within the realm of what may be called *empirics*, as distinct from the realms of *aesthetics* and *ethics*. Even so, it must be admitted that the outcomes of some types of research in education are best evaluated by the subjective opinion of the group.

K. Lovell
K. S. Lawson
The University
Leeds

CHAPTER 1

The acquisition of knowledge and the aims of research

Methods of acquiring knowledge

Throughout the period of recorded history it appears that man has attempted both to obtain more knowledge about his environment and to appraise its significance. Indeed, it seems as if it is in the very nature of man to try to make his world, and life itself, meaningful and significant. To this end he has strived ceaselessly. Furthermore, he has also tried to extend his knowledge in order to improve his way of life, thereby rendering it more comfortable and more secure.

But across the centuries there have been changes in the ways in which man has obtained his information, and we shall get a better understanding of the methods he now uses if we also look at his earlier attempts. However, it will be seen later that even in the natural sciences, which are concerned with events within the matter-energy system, there are still no methods for obtaining 'absolute truth' or 'certainty'. In the social sciences, which included education, there is an added difficulty. Human beings, as distinct from natural phenomena, may not be contained wholly within the matter-energy system, in the sense that human activity is partly determined by psychical forces such as 'mind' or 'will' (cf. Burt 1968)* or even by transcendental influences. It is possible, then, that the knowledge which is eventually obtainable about human beings—even if we had a great deal more than we have at present—may never enable us to predict

* The references are given on p. 148 ff.

human activity with the same precision as we can sometimes predict natural phenomena. This difficult but important point must be recognized at the outset.

The methods which man has used, and still uses, in obtaining knowledge are now discussed under a number of headings.

PERSONAL EXPERIENCE

Early man's observations and experience led him to appreciate that the part of the sky in which the sun rose and set varied. Likewise his experience led him to know where certain animals were likely to be found, and when it was time to plant his seeds. Modern man also acquires knowledge via personal experience—for example, when he learns to grow, say, particular varieties of roses, or when he learns where in a sea loch fish are likely to be found at a given time of year. Again, in the classroom a teacher may find that a particular teaching method may be very successful with a certain group of pupils. But there also are many dangers in appealing to personal experience. For example, observations and records of what was experienced or performed may be poorly made; generalizations may be drawn on insufficient evidence or too few examples; incorrect conclusions may follow through prejudice; and evidence may be left out because it was not consonant with earlier experiences. Finally, there is always the danger of failing to recognize which were the salient features of the situation and which were irrelevant. Some of the dangers of relying too heavily on personal experience are well expressed by Bacon (quoted by Beveridge 1957) when he warned of the snags of depending upon personal impressions: 'The human understanding is most excited by that which strikes and enters the mind at once. . . . It then begins almost imperceptibly to conceive and suppose that everything is similar to the few objects which have taken impression in the mind.'

AUTHORITY

Man seems to have some predilection for authority and authority figures. Perhaps this reflects a sense of basic insecurity. In earlier centuries he turned to priests and kings for help and knowledge. Today preliterate man may turn to tribal chief or witch doctor who are thought to have knowledge and power not available to all, while literate man tends to turn to the expert.

In everyday life a certain amount of knowledge is handed down by parents, teachers, scientists, for example, and must be taken on trust, since life is too short to test the validity of every view that is held. At the same time it is important to realize that because information has been given by parents, leaders or rulers, that because certain knowledge has been handed down through the ages and is widely believed, it does not necessarily follow that it is true. For a long time it was the generally held view, including that of the Church, that the sun revolved around the earth. In more recent times generations of medical men believed that blood letting and the application of leeches to the body increased the patient's chances of recovery. A hundred years from now it is more than likely that many of the views now held about the educative process will be regarded as erroneous. On the other hand, however, innumerable views handed down by authority do stand up to the test of time. For example, medical men have, for thousands of years, used extracts from plants such as deadly nightshade and purple foxglove. We now know that these extracts contain valuable drugs like atropine and digitalis whose worth has been consistently shown, so that they remain important forms of treatment of certain disorders to the present day.

Generally speaking, the expert is better informed in his field than other people because of the level of his intelligence and his training and experience. Thus we take seriously the views of, say, the bacteriologist and the civil engineer. But sometimes experts disagree among themselves; for example, psychiatrists will sometimes differ regarding the state of mind of the accused person in a court. Indeed, disagreement is often found among experts in the social sciences, including education. Thus care must always be taken about the credentials of the expert and a check must be made to see if he is knowledgeable about the particular point or points at issue. It is also important to investigate the evidence and arguments of experts. Finally, it is essential not to accept, without question, a particular viewpoint for all time.

While, then, it is clear that each generation cannot start from scratch in its search for knowledge, an appeal to authority in the form of tradition or expert may not always result in the truth being obtained.

DEDUCTIVE REASONING

In ancient Greece the deductive method of reasoning was developed into a highly refined art and was greatly prized. Indeed, the syllogism was frequently used for centuries as a method of acquiring knowledge. This is made up of three statements or propositions, the first two statements being called *premises*, as they provide the basis or evidence for the conclusion of the argument, which is given in the third statement. The following is an example of a *categorical* syllogism; i.e. it is composed of clear, definite, categorical statements:

Human beings cannot live without oxygen.
Children under five years of age are human beings.
Therefore children under five years of age cannot live without oxygen.

A syllogism does not have to be made from categorical statements. When our thinking or knowledge is less certain, we can have either the *hypothetical* or the *alternative* syllogism. An example of each is given here:

Hypothetical syllogism

If it continues to rain, the valley is in danger of being flooded.
It continues to rain.
Therefore the valley is in danger of being flooded.

Alternative syllogism

Either John will be allowed to take the course or he will leave school.
John is not to be allowed to take the course.
Therefore John will leave school.

Deductive reasoning is used in everyday life to solve a host of problems. The detective and doctor use it, for example, when they search among evidence and symptoms respectively, select items which appeared to be unrelated at first, and then bring them together in such a way that they logically yield a conclusion. Thus if footprints of one size were found beneath a window, and footprints of another size and tyre marks were found in the drive to the house, it could be deduced that one person stayed by the car while another burgled the house.

Note carefully, however, that even in the case of the categorical syllogism—that is, the instance in which we are most certain of our knowledge—the syllogism only enables us to deduce the consequences of what was already known. Thus, while it permits logical deductions from known facts, it does not yield any really new knowledge.

Another point to note is that if one of the premises is untrue, the conclusion will be false. Consider the syllogism:

All students in colleges of education have three GCE 'A' level passes (major premise).
Miss X is a student in such a college.
Therefore Miss X possesses three GCE 'A' level passes.

The major premise was false, so the conclusion is also untrue.

It can thus be seen that while deduction is a useful tool for obtaining certain kinds of information, it must not be relied upon exclusively. The truth of the premises must be examined, and the limitation of deduction in respect of the extension of new knowledge clearly recognized. Indeed, most discoveries are not made through the use of deductive logic. Francis Bacon (1561–1626), whose work we shall mention again in the next section, wrote as long ago as 1605: 'Men are rather beholden . . . generally to chance, or anything else, than to logic, for the invention of arts and sciences'.

INDUCTIVE REASONING

By the sixteenth century the Aristotelian method of syllogistic reasoning was being increasingly attacked. Of particular note in this connection was Francis Bacon, who argued against the practice, prevalent for centuries, of drawing conclusions from authoritative premises. As an alternative he maintained that man should, by careful observation, collect his own data and use these as the basis for making generalizations.

Once again there are difficulties, for it is rarely possible to count all the instances of a given class of events or objects because of the time and effort involved. For example, it would not be feasible to measure the heights of all the ten-year-olds in the British Isles. If one could do so, it would be possible to make a true statement or generalization about such children within this geographical area. It would be an example of perfect induction. Such complete enumeration, however, is rarely possible. In nearly all real-life situations the scientist can observe only some instances of the class, and then he has to draw conclusions concerning all similar instances. For example, the heights of 100 samples each containing thirty ten-year-olds could be ascertained without much difficulty and from this a generalization would have to be made about the heights of all ten-year-olds living in the

British Isles. This is an example of imperfect induction, for in making an inference about the whole of a population after sampling relatively few of its members, one does not necessarily obtain knowledge which is true. The size of the samples and the extent to which they are representative of the whole population limits the degree to which the conclusions are sound. If the sampling is unsatisfactory, some of the instances unobserved may not be consonant with the conclusions drawn from the observations made. Thus imperfect induction does not necessarily give the truth; rather it yields conclusions which are true in varying degrees of probability. On the other hand, inductive reasoning, unlike deductive reasoning, does give knowledge that is not present, even by implication, in one of the premises—that is, in one of the observations. The inductive method does not, of course, lead *immediately* to generalizations and concepts which cannot be directly derived from first-hand observation. Thus Einstein (quoted by Beveridge 1957) emphasized this point when he wrote: 'There is no inductive method which could lead to the fundamental concepts of physics. Failure to understand this fact constituted the basic philosophical error of so many investigators of the nineteenth century.'

ONE CURRENT METHOD

If mere random observations are made, one tends to become burdened with snippets of information. Somehow man had to elaborate a practical method of selecting and handling his observations so that he could make some sense out of them and so that they would yield reliable and significant knowledge. Thus from around the seventeenth century eminent men such as Isaac Newton and others who followed him made use of a synthesis of reason and observation to give a method now frequently used in scientific research. In essence man has to reflect on his own thinking when using this approach, and

Dewey (1933) has indicated the main stages that thought passes through when man attempts to discover new knowledge by this means.

In the first stage some problem is encountered which cannot be solved or explained at once. Next, such observations are made and such facts gathered as appear to be relevant so that the problem can be located and defined more precisely. This is a very important stage, for the care with which these data are collected can markedly affect the conclusions reached. Third, the investigator must, after studying the data, try to make some intelligent guesses to explain the relationships between the facts—that is, he formulates suggested solutions to the problems. These solutions or hypotheses are at the heart of the method. The ability with which a person can produce useful hypotheses depends both upon the quality of his thinking and upon the amount of previously acquired knowledge which is relevant to the problem under investigation. Stage four involves working out the consequences if these hypotheses were true; this clearly involves deductive reasoning. In the last stage the investigator looks for evidence of the consequences that should follow if the hypotheses were true. So the research worker establishes which hypotheses are congruent with the observed facts.

This general method is often called 'the scientific method', although whether this is a good name for it is a moot point. Note, too, that the investigator's thinking moves to and fro across these stages and he does not always follow the stages in the order given above. In short, he frequently shifts between collecting information, hypothesizing to explain his data, finding out what are the logical consequences of his hypotheses, and obtaining more data to test the truth of these.

As an example of this general method consider the oscillation of a simple pendulum. The investigator is given a length of string suspended from a hook and a number of different weights which he can attach to the lower end. He can vary the length of the string, the weight used for the bob, the impetus imparted to the bob and the height from which it is dropped. After experimentation and the collection of a certain number of facts, the investigator must come up with some bright ideas as to which of the variables is responsible for determining the time of swing of the bob. Let us suppose that his experimentation leads him to hypothesize that it is the length of the string which controls the period of oscillation of the pendulum. If his hypothesis is true, then it follows that if he holds the other variables constant and changes only the length of the string, the expected variations in the period of swing should be in evidence. If evidence congruent with the deduced consequences of his hypothesis is not obtained, then he must look to his hypothesis again.

This general method of acquiring knowledge is more flexible than the other methods described, and it encourages doubt and experiment until evidence is obtained which is consonant with the hypothesis advanced. Moreover, if fresh evidence arises at a later date which is no longer congruent with the deduced consequences of a particular hypothesis, that hypothesis must be modified or abandoned. What has been broadly called the scientific method has been very valuable in establishing new knowledge in the natural sciences, and it has also helped social scientists, including educationists, to gain insight into their problems. But it cannot answer questions involving moral or value judgements. Indeed, man has no one method for acquiring the knowledge necessary to answer all his questions.

Three other points must be made. First, it must be noted that now in the latter half of the twentieth century it is realized that the scientific method does not lead us to 'eternal truth' but rather to systematic doubt. This view is in contrast to that held at the end of the last century, when it was widely thought that there was no way to a knowledge of the universe except through the scientific method. Indeed, this point is of such great importance that it will be raised again later when we deal with the role of theory in research. It is sufficient here to quote from Thompson (1961): 'The scientific method is not a royal road leading to discovery in research . . . but rather a collection of pieces of advice . . . which may help to guide the explorer in his passage through the jungle of arbitrary facts'. Second, there are those who argue that the scientific method is not just one single method of attack equally applicable to the natural and social sciences, archaeology, etc. Such persons take the view that sciences differ greatly from one another and that it is not possible to find a rule applicable to them all. Against this is the view that the scientific method is a general method which merely becomes modified in varying ways to suit different disciplines. Third, underpinning the scientific method are certain assumptions both about nature and about the psychology of man. It is not our intention to examine these assumptions here, but it must be recognized that they exist.

SERENDIPITY AND INTUITION

Sometimes when a particular piece of knowledge is being looked for, something quite different but of equal or greater value is found. Such an accidental discovery is serendipity. Although chance has resulted in many important discoveries, they are too rare to be relied upon. A well-known example of the happy accident occurred to Alexander Fleming around 1930. He was studying the growth of bacteria in a small dish and found that the bacteria stopped growing when they were surrounded and killed by mould which had got into the dish by accident. In this way penicillin, from which the mould had come, became such an important antibiotic.

It seems necessary for the fortuitous event to happen to a person who is both a trained observer and has the necessary knowledge to appreciate its significance. The position was well put by Pasteur when he made the point that in the field of observation, chance favoured the prepared mind.

On other occasions new knowledge comes to the research worker through intuition, using the term not in the Piagetian sense, but in the sense of hunch, inspiration, illumination or insight. Sometimes the new knowledge has arisen when the related subject matter was being consciously considered, while on other occasions the investigator was not consciously aware of the problem at all. Perhaps the most famous example of this general type was the discovery by Archimedes of the principle that carries his name. Although intuition is more frequently reported by scientists than is serendipity, it, too, has its limitations. As in the case of chance, intuition seems fruitful only with the 'prepared mind', since before intuition operates there has usually been much preliminary thinking about the topic. Although the research worker may have an intuition when, say, walking, boating or in bed, when he does experience it the solution to the problem or the new knowledge generally comes instantly and clearly.

The general aims of research

This chapter opened by making the point that man seems impelled both to explain to himself the nature of his environment and to apply his knowledge to make life more comfortable and secure. So we find that early man proposed all manner of explanations—some now regarded as useful, some as crude, some as nonsensical—for the phenomena he experienced. He also sought knowledge so that he could control his environment and so minimize the effects of natural disasters like famines and floods. Finally he consulted his astrologers, priests or wise men who were thought to be able to predict the future. By so doing he hoped to know of the outcome of his actions or be able to take action to avoid calamity. While we may now look upon the efforts of early man to explain, control and predict as poor ones, it is important to realize that twentieth-century man has the same aims although he uses more sophisticated methods to attain them. Moreover, in later centuries our methods may be looked upon as relatively inefficient. However, the major aims of research are now considered in turn.

EXPLANATION

Collecting data, putting names to objects or items, or even categorizing data is often a first and necessary step in research. But is it essential to move beyond mere description of phenomena as, for example, 'Some twelve-year-olds read like some seven-year-olds' or 'Pennies sink in water', and provide explanations for the phenomena. The scientist wants to know the reasons for their occurrence. Having found possible causes for a particular happening or state of affairs, he has to build a generalization that will explain how the factors influencing the happening or state behave in order that he can relate the factors to a wider body of knowledge. Making a generalization or building a conceptual framework provides an explanation for the phenomenon. Moreover, the scientist wants a generalization that not merely explains the past, or is postdictive, but one that is also predictive.

The conceptual framework that the research worker aims to erect will explain as much as possible. The greater the explanatory power of the generalization or conceptual framework, the greater is its value.*

CONTROL

The scientist often wishes to control conditions which have an adverse effect on the human race. Thus he wishes to control, say,

* Piaget (1968) suggests that in psychology seven types of explanatory models are used.

the spread of malaria, or the conditions which lead a child to be backward in reading. But before control can be exercised, sound and extensive knowledge must be available. To date, man has been relatively more successful in controlling what may be broadly called physical phenomena than in controlling social phenomena. In the latter the variables are more complex and we have less certain knowledge, as we shall see later.

PREDICTION

As stated above, the research worker wants predictive and not postdictive generalizations so that his conceptual framework will operate in new situations. In the natural sciences research has often been highly successful in elaborating such generalizations so that prediction is well-nigh certain. For example, the planet Pluto was predicted as existing years before it was actually identified. On the other hand, weather forecasts, scholastic failure or success, or consequent conditions in the social sciences can be predicted less accurately.

It is important to remember, however, that prediction in science does not necessarily mean foretelling the future as in the case of weather forecasting or estimating the likelihood of scholastic progress. The scientist is often, if not more frequently, concerned with a widely based conceptual framework or theory which will predict. For example, since in human beings the gene responsible for colour blindness is carried on the Y chromosome and the Y chromosome determines the sex of the child, it can be predicted that far fewer girls than boys will be afflicted with this handicap.

CHAPTER 2

Problems and theory in different areas of research

In this chapter four broad issues are dealt with. First a note is made of some of the differences between the natural and the social sciences, since education, in so far as it is one of the sciences at all, is one of the latter group. Second, the place and value of theory in research must be briefly discussed. Although teachers have not always felt sympathetic to educational theories, largely in the writers' view because the theories have been poor ones, the role of theory must be clearly recognized. Third,the characteristics of different types of research activities get a brief mention, while fourth, there is a discussion of some of the problems which are specific to educational research.

The natural and the social sciences

Explanation, control and prediction is often possible in the natural sciences. Indeed, the probability in respect of prediction sometimes approaches certainty. In the social sciences, however, the aims of research are not so easily realized. While some progress has been made, there are persons who believe that explanation, control and prediction will never reach the high levels attained in the natural sciences. Others argue that, given enough time, the social sciences will eventually be on a par with the natural sciences in these respects, although agreeing that the former lag behind the latter at the moment. If we look at the two groups of sciences we may note the following:

a) In the natural sciences the research worker often has few variables to deal with although this is not always the case, as for example, in weather forecasting. But at least all the variables are amenable to objective measurements made within the matter-energy system. However, in the social sciences we have to deal with such variables as, say, intelligence, temperament, social relationships within the classroom or attitudes of parents. Not only are the variables difficult to assess (as will be mentioned again later) but they interact in subtle ways. In short, the social scientist has far more complex situations to deal with.

b) It is not always possible to observe, directly, the salient features operating in human situations. For example, one cannot observe directly a child's past history, and one has either to rely upon written records of his characteristics and behaviour made at the time, or on anecdotes. Again, it is possible to sample a child's vocabulary with some objectivity but difficult to determine his motives or the intensity of his dreams. If a child says 'I do not understand' or 'I feel lonely', the observer has either to accept the child's description of the state of his consciousness, or he must interpret the child's state in terms of how he himself feels in a similar state.

c) Situations that involve human beings are to some extent unique, in that particular persons each with his own background are thinking or behaving in a specific situation. To some extent, then, it is difficult to make wide generalizations from this unique situation; there is too great a danger of over-generalizing. Furthermore, each situation in which human beings find themselves is to some extent a learning situation for them. They are slightly different beings after having had the experience. Thus a child learns something through taking a test or examination, and he does not behave in quite the same way if he takes it again. In the natural sciences, however, situations are often completely repeatable. For example, electrons are like one another, and always behave in the same way under given conditions.

d) In the social sciences the research worker's background,

interests, prejudices and values tend to determine both what he observes and the judgements he makes on his observations. In the natural sciences, however, when studying, say, the viscosity or salinity of sea water, he is less likely to be influenced in this way—or be influenced to a lesser extent. Again, when the natural scientist formulates a hypothesis to explain his findings, any subsequent generalization will not cause the phenomena to change their character. In the social sciences, however, the situation may be very different. If, for example, it was hypothesized that condition X affects, adversely, children's educational progress, there may be such a hue and cry that condition X may be far less frequently found and the whole situation changed.

In spite of what has just been said, and of the remark made in chapter 1 that human activity may in part be determined by transcendental influences, *groups* of human beings do display some stable characteristics which may be predicted with a high degree of probability. For example, it is possible to calculate the probable yield from a given tax on a specific article although individuals can decide whether or not to purchase the article. Again, insurance actuaries cannot predict when a particular individual will have an accident, but they can assess the probability of such an occurrence for large groups fairly accurately. So it should be noted that while in educational research it may occasionally prove possible to predict with some accuracy the course of activity of a particular individual (more frequently it will be impossible to do so), prediction for groups may reach somewhat higher levels of probability.

The role of theory in research

We have already said that the collection of facts is only the first step in research. The investigator must search among his facts, spot relevant relationships between the facts, or supply a concept that will put the facts into some kind of meaningful pattern. As we have seen, a hypothesis when accepted will explain a limited number of facts and the interrelations between them. A generalization is, as its name implies, a hypothesis of greater generality. A theory—as the term is used by the scientist*—explains even more facts and the interrelations between them and is of still greater generality, although theories themselves can range from the simple to the more sophisticated. Finally there are laws, which have the greatest scope and generality. It is, of course, the aim of science to elaborate laws of the greatest possible comprehensiveness. In the social sciences generalizations can sometimes be made, theories arise less frequently, while laws can be formulated very rarely indeed at present. Note, however, that even laws have to be amended when new evidence is obtained which is not consonant with the law; or the unchanged law must be shown to operate in certain circumstances only.

It is important to stress that good theories are not 'airy fairy'; they are not imaginations of the dreamer's mind; they do not originate merely through reflecting in arm-chairs. A theory is built upon facts which were collected in some way in the first instance. The investigator then searches among them, makes intelligent guesses as to how the facts are ordered; adds missing ideas or links; puts forward a hypothesis; deduces what consequences should follow from the hypotheses and looks for further facts which are consonant or otherwise with the deductions; builds a wider generalization or conceptual framework on more facts; and eventually elaborates a theory. Theories, let it be stressed, are solidly based on evidence. And they are important practical tools which enable man to advance his knowledge still further, as will be shown later.

Once a theoretical framework has been elaborated we know what facts to look for to confirm or deny the theory; also we have

* Throughout the book the term 'theory' is used in the sense in which the scientist employs it.

a conceptual framework inside which our evidence can be discussed. In connection with the former point it is interesting to note that in the junior school children pick up facts almost indiscriminately. In science they gather facts as a magpie gathers 'bits and pieces'. In adolescence there is a change. When hypothetico-deductive thinking is available, the pupil knows what evidence to look for to help him decide upon the truth or untruth of the hypothesis or theory in question.

Again a theory permits the classification of facts as in, say, the classification of plants in botany. It also permits the elaboration of new concepts as in the case of, say, the concept of 'mental structures' in Piaget's developmental theory. Finally the theory often enables one to make predictions which are consonant with the theory but which have not yet been observed; also it allows one to point out areas where knowledge is lacking and further research is needed. For example, a given theory could be shown to be relevant when considering rural children, but the data on which it is based could make it self evident that the theory has not, as yet, been shown to hold true for urban pupils.

In spite of the strong case that has been made for the role of theory in research, it will be appreciated that a theory must be amended or abandoned when new facts are discovered that cannot be accommodated by it. Alternatively, it may be subsumed under a wider, more embracing theory, when it is realized that the situation which is contained by the theory is but one instance of a more general case. Theories generated by the means that we have indicated do not lead to 'eternal truth'; rather they should be looked upon as useful conceptual frameworks which are adequate for present purposes. K. R. Popper (1959) aptly described the situation when he wrote: 'Science does not rest upon rock bottom. The bold structure of its theories rises, as it were, above a swamp. It is like a building erected on piles. . . . We simply stop when we are satisfied that they the [piles] are firm enough to carry the structure, at least for the time being.'

We stated earlier that teachers have often distrusted theory—at least the theories that they have been offered. They ask for 'practical advice' or 'practical men', not theory. This is because they have been given, and have become accustomed to what may be called 'layman's theories'. The theory of the scientist and that of the layman both purport to offer generalizations, yet they derive their theories quite differently. The former elaborates his theory through carefully established facts and states it in precise terms. The latter makes his theories too from his observations—often not carefully made and recorded—but without making a careful analysis of the interrelations between the facts and pursuing the further stages in theorizing which we have seen to be so necessary. Not only are layman's theories easily and quickly elaborated, but they are easily communicated to others in layman's terms. Educational policies and practices have been, and still are, often based on popular theories, and one of the aims of the research worker in education is to move educational theories of folklore status to theories of scientific status. This is a slow process, and children have to be educated as well as we can do so until more powerful theories are available.

Construct, model, theory

In the literature of the social scientists the term *construct* will be met. This indicates an idea which the social scientist creates out of his imagination and which helps him to think about underlying mechanisms to account for human thought and behaviour. In essence constructs give a plausible explanation of the consistency of human behaviour. Thus intelligence, verbal ability, spatial-mechanical ability are all hypothetical constructs. They cannot in themselves be seen; only the outcomes of the resulting thinking can be observed. Hypothetical constructs are used just as frequently by natural scientists to think about mechanisms that will explain natural phenomena, e.g. electric field.

Another term used by both natural and social scientists is *model.* This indicates a likeness of representation of certain aspects of complex phenomena made by using objects or symbols which in some way resemble the phenomena being modelled. A model is essentially an analogy. A replica model looks like the object or phenomena, whereas in a symbolic model abstract symbols such as those involved in, say, mathematical equations or graphic representations are made. A good example of a model in psychology is Guilford's (1967) model of the intellect. In practice it is not always easy to draw a line between constructs and models.

Since a model is analogical, it may contain certain facts which are not in strict accord with the real facts, whereas a theory should be able to contain all the observed data but no incompatable facts—or the theory is not valid. While, then, both models and theories are conceptual frameworks inside which we can think about our phenomena, we ought, perhaps, to judge theories by the extent to which they are true, and models by the extent to which they are useful.

The types of research

If we look at science in a broad sense, it is possible to formulate a threefold classification of research activities providing it is clearly recognized that there can be no hard-and-fast division into these three categories. First, there is what one may call basic or fundamental research. This is, perhaps, research in the classical sense. It includes original investigation for the advancement of knowledge of the subject matter and does not necessarily involve any concern for its immediate or practical application. In mathematics, for example, there have been numerous instances where research findings have been unused for many years and then suddenly brought into prominence as they were relevant to the solution of some current problem. Second, there is applied research. This research is directed towards the application of new knowledge to solve day-to-day problems. It is necessary to stress, particularly in Britain, that basic and applied research, while differing in the goals they hope to achieve, are not differentiated by complexity—intellectual or otherwise. Third, there is what may be called developmental research. This involves the systematic use of scientific knowledge for the production of methods, processes, systems and useful devices, but not involving problems which are specific to questions of design and production engineering.

When we discuss the division of educational research later in this chapter, we shall see that something of the above framework has been maintained, although it has not been kept in its entirety.

Research in education

So far little has been said that is specific to research in education. It was important to keep the discussion to research in general so that educational research could be seen in better perspective. Now some aspects of the topic of educational research will be discussed.

DEFINITION OF EDUCATIONAL RESEARCH

It is virtually impossible to give a definition of the term 'educational research' which would command universal acceptance, as there are innumerable meanings that can be given to the word 'education'. Two definitions are given below, although it is not pretended that they are altogether satisfactory:

Educational research may be defined broadly as any systematic

> striving for understanding activated by a need or sensed difficulty directed towards some complex educational problem of more than immediate personal concern and stated in problematic form (cf. Harris 1960, *Encyclopedia of Educational Research*).

> Thus we can say research [educational] should always denote careful, critical, and exhaustive investigation to discover new facts which will test a hypothesis, revise accepted conclusions, or contribute positive values to society in general (cf. McAshan 1963).

The first definition suggests that educational research should be systematic rather than casual and that ideally it should arise out of carefully formulated problems. Thus the topic 'The age, training and experience of junior school teachers' might be a useful area of investigation; it is an area in which problems might be formulated, but the title as it stands presents no problem. This definition clearly accords with all that has been said so far in this book about research. The second definition is consonant with the first, but it introduces a new element. It suggests that value judgements are of importance in educational research; this point will be raised again later.

It must be stressed, however, that research in education is greatly dependent upon research in other subject disciplines. It relies greatly on findings in human development, psychology and sociology, and, where cross-cultural studies are concerned, on anthropology.

TYPES OF EDUCATIONAL RESEARCH

It is suggested that at present educational research can be thought of in terms of three broad divisions. But these are not mutually exclusive and sometimes a piece of research may fall into more than one of these categories.

1. A study of what is actually happening at the present time in any area of the educational field. Examples of such studies could be 'Laboratory provision in comprehensive schools'; 'The number of immigrant pupils, and their country of origin, entering the schools of a LEA in the past twelve months'. It is virtually the collection of facts, and such studies can vary from the simple counting of heads to more complex investigations like those which will be illustrated later in this book. Such surveys are often necessary for the purposes of educational planning. It might be objected that the collection of facts, important as they are, is not research in the sense in which it has been considered so far. To some extent this objection must be accepted, but the hope is that the facts will often lead to deeper considerations leading on to more fundamental research. Indeed, such is frequently the case as the interrelations between the facts become analysed.

2. Education has to deal with very real day-to-day problems and much of what is considered as educational research can be classified as developmental in nature. It is the kind of research that has been sponsored by the Schools Council and the Nuffield Foundation, and is often concerned with both syllabus and curriculum reform and with an examination of the aims and methods of the courses of study decided upon. In short, such research involves the re-appraisal of curriculum and teaching, and is likely to be a continuous process as young people have to be educated to take their place in a changing technological society. This type of research should always rest firmly upon what is known of cognitive and other aspects of human development.

3. The third category embraces basic or fundamental research. Here there is the finding of new facts, the elaboration of new theories or the re-appraisal of old ones. Knowledge of many

disciplines are nearly always involved. In this type of research the investigator feels free to tackle any problem which he thinks to be of importance, and he does not have to be concerned with whether or not his findings can necessarily be put to immediate use in practice. Findings in basic research may, however, provide vital knowledge as a link or as a tool in a practical situation some years later, even when they cannot be used at once. Some psychologists, for example, who work on aspects of learning theory would say that, at present, their findings have no relevance to the classroom situation although they hope that their research will one day be of value to the teacher.

Basic research is not altogether popular among educationists as it demands skilled man-power, is time consuming and expensive, while, as we have just stated, the findings often cannot be made to yield immediate practical results. It must, however, be remembered that the production of powerful explanatory, controlling and predictive theories in the social sciences, including education, is a slow business as the subject is so complex. But if one ignores basic research there is a danger that education is likely to be unduly influenced by pressure groups, by dogma based on whim, by personal preference, or by experience based on limited samples of children. When experimental education does not have a theoretical base, it can have a spurious sense of adequacy. There is also the danger, if basic research is neglected, of failing to build a corpus of workers experienced and confident in handling complex research designs and projects.

AIMS OF EDUCATIONAL RESEARCH

The aims of research in education are the same as those of research in science generally. This can be illustrated by a practical example. Although standards of reading have improved considerably since the end of the Second World War, there remains a sizeable group of children who are backward in this basic skill. We need good theories that will (a) offer satisfactory explanations of the various causes of reading failure, (b) predict which children are likely to have problems in reading, and (c) enable us to control the variables involved so that we can either prevent backwardness in reading or elaborate techniques which will ameliorate the condition in a far more effective manner than we can at the moment.

Taylor (1966) suggests that what separates educational research from other research is the centrality of practical judgements, which involve values, in the former. He is right to stress the importance of such judgements in educational research, but in our view, investigators in other branches of the social sciences and in the natural sciences must also be sensitive to the needs of their societies and to the existing climate of opinion, and make value judgements concerning the areas of knowledge in which they will work so that they are also at times concerned with solving problems that will help man to act 'better'. No research—regardless of the field of operation—is, of course, independent of value judgements in the sense that decisions have to be made as to what, in the light of current opinion and knowledge, are worth-while topics, what is feasible, and what is likely to bring practical benefit to mankind sooner or later. As for what is 'worth-while' and what will bring 'benefit', there may be much debate.

In the same paper Taylor also draws attention to the fact that some philosophers argue that the central problems of education involve ethical and moral judgements, and research in the sense indicated in this book plays only a minor role. Such philosophers take an extreme view, which does not gain wide acceptance. Nevertheless, it must be recognized that educational research is best fostered by those investigators who do have some knowledge of the practical judgements and values which decide what should or should not be done in educational practice.

FURTHER POINTS TO CONSIDER IN EDUCATIONAL RESEARCH

Let us return again to the fact that many teachers dislike theory. It must, of course, be accepted that the scientific method, or any other method described in this book, does not concern itself with value judgements. But once the goals of education have been decided, there are innumerable problems where the techniques of scientific research can be applied. If such application is not made, then teachers must continue on the basis of personal experience, authority, trial and error and the like in coming to decisions on many matters. Such methods may or may not be of value, as we have seen. But when theories have been elaborated in the way we have indicated (they may range from, say, theories of learning to theories of reading failure), there will be no gap between theory and practice, for the former is built upon facts. That teachers have been offered many poor theories in the past, and are likely to go on experiencing poor theories for some time yet, should not blind them to the fact that the predictions of a good theory will leave the mere 'practical' man far behind.

It must be stressed, however, that much research now carried out in education is based on no precise theoretical position; frequently hypotheses are not explicitly advanced nor evidence sought which is consonant or otherwise with consequences deduced from them, although the investigators may well have a general idea about the ways in which the variables are related. Educational research is still very much at the stage of gathering facts even if quite sophisticated techniques are used to analyse them. Such researches are largely *ex post facto* studies. In research reported in the relevant literature, readers must not be disappointed if no precise theories or clear hypotheses are always to be found when they read the original reports. This warning is necessary after the stress placed in this chapter on the role of theory in research, and in view of the fact that they will meet critics of research which is undertaken without a theoretical basis.

In order to encourage teachers to look critically at research findings a number of questions are given below which they should ask themselves about a particular study. Other points will be made in later chapters. These questions alert the reader at this stage of the book as to the kind of points he should look for to judge if a given piece of research is likely to be of value.

Does the topic, however limited, appear to be of likely help in attempting to solve some important or theoretical issue?
Is the problem stated in terms which are clear and free of all ambiguity?
Is the relevant literature adequately reviewed?
If the facts are to be collected, does the investigator have a clear goal or goals which indicate to him which facts are likely to be relevant?
Is there a clear statement of testable hypotheses?
If there is such a statement, are the assumptions on which they are predicted made clear?
Are the consequences which follow the hypotheses stated lucidly so that there is no doubt about what is to be tested?
If no hypotheses are stated, does it appear that the investigator has some idea about the way in which the variables are interrelated and that he is proceeding in a manner consistent with some goal?
Are the variables used in the research stated in terms which make them open to precise measurement?
Will the instruments and techniques of measurement used produce reliable and valid information?
Will the research design give data that will yield information necessary to test the hypotheses?
Is there any danger of the investigator over-generalizing from small and unrepresentative samples?

Does the analysis merely reflect the observed or surface conditions, or does it delve into the interrelations between the variables?

Is the acceptance or rejection of the hypotheses consonant with the statistical evidence?

Have factors which might have affected the results but which could not be controlled, been clearly indicated in the 'write-up' of the results?

CHAPTER 3

Descriptive research

Procedures

Before much progress can be made in solving educational problems, descriptions of the phenomena must be obtained by means of *descriptive research.* Early developments in educational research, therefore —as in the early stages of other disciplines— have been concerned with making accurate assessments of the incidence, distribution and relationships of the phenomena in the field. Even today there are areas of education about which little is known, and there is a need for research to uncover something of the nature of the factors which brought about the states of affairs or contributed to their continuance. For example, to solve problems about children, school organization or the teaching of a subject, information or facts must be gathered about what exists. The nature of prevailing conditions, educational practices and existing attitudes must often be determined and the activities, objects and persons described.

Descriptive research, however, does not consist solely of routine fact gathering, although this is an important aspect of this type of research. It should also seek to determine the degree to which underlying factors exist in given situations and under given conditions, and estimate their relative importance. Furthermore, descriptive research can be used to identify which underlying factors have some relationship or link between them, although it may be that no assumptions can be made that the relationship is one of cause and effect. Thus research of this nature may not answer basic questions, but it does allow for the gathering of information which serves as a basis for future research founded, perhaps, on some tentative hypothesis.

Descriptive research does not involve the use of experiments *per se*. As already stated, it seeks to uncover the nature of the factors involved in a given situation, it seeks to determine the degree in which they exist, and it attempts to discover the links or relationships which exist between the factors. Descriptive research, whilst built on tabulation, must go beyond the mere gathering and tabulating of data, as we stressed earlier. It involves an element of interpretation of the meaning or significance of what is described Whilst many research reports demonstrate the skill with which observations have been carried out, many reveal that little insight has been shown in the interpretation of the results of the research.

In carrying out studies of a descriptive nature, research workers ought not merely to present subjective impressions and data based on casual observations of phenomena. As in other types of research it is necessary to follow carefully defined procedures.

1. The area under investigation must be examined, the specific problem defined, and the data to be collected must be carefully described.
2. Hypotheses must be stated together with the assumptions upon which the hypotheses are based. In some instances, however, where the research is of an exploratory type it is not always possible to state a hypothesis.
3. The selection of appropriate subjects and a description of the procedures to be followed when carrying out the research are further necessary steps.
4. The research instruments or tools or techniques to be used in the collection of data must be specified and reasons given for their choice. If new techniques have been devised, detailed information should be given of their construction.
5. Finally the results must be described, analysed and interpreted in clear precise terms, and suggestions made for further research.

Research workers ought, therefore, even when carrying out work at an elementary level, to seek more than bare description of data. They should not be mere tabulators. Evidence ought to be collected on the basis of some hypothesis or theory, summarized carefully, and analysed in an endeavour to draw meaningful generalizations which will increase knowledge.

Descriptive research, then, describes and interprets what is. It is concerned with conditions that exist, practices that prevail, beliefs and attitudes that are held, processes that are on-going, and trends that are developing.

Before carrying out a descriptive research study consideration must be given to the collection of data. A first step is to consider the number of units which exist in the problem area and to make decisions as to whether the study should be concerned with all these units or with only some of them. Thus all the teachers teaching in the primary schools of a local education authority may constitute a population. If the population is small—for example, a class of children—it may be feasible to include all the units (in this case children) in the study. However, if the population is large—for example, in the case of the number of children attending school in the United Kingdom—it may be feasible to include only a proportion or a sample of the total number in the study. If the latter course is followed, it is important that the sample should accurately represent the characteristics of the population if generalizations based upon the data obtained from them are to be applied to the population as a whole. The selection of such a representative sample presents many difficulties; these are discussed more fully in chapter 8.

Data may be collected by a variety of means in descriptive research. It is a common misconception that few data-gathering techniques can be utilized. In fact many instruments can be used, although the question as to which instruments are used in a specific investigation depends upon the nature of the problem and the hypotheses to be tested. Each instrument is appropriate for acquiring particular data, and sometimes several instruments will have to be used. It is the task of the investigator to examine the various tools available and to choose those most suited to his purpose. If the existing ones do not meet his specific needs, he may supplement or modify them or even construct his own. An example of the modification of an instrument is Bigg's (1962) modification of the Sarason Anxiety Scales, and at the time of writing the NFER is developing new attitude scales to investigate attitudes to science (National Foundation for Educational Research 1968a).

The instruments used in research in the behavioural sciences generally will be discussed in chapters 5, 6 and 7. Of these, questionnaires, interviews and appraisal instruments are those most frequently used in descriptive research.

Questionnaires are widely used to obtain facts about current conditions and practices and to make inquiries concerning attitudes and opinions. For some studies or certain phases of them, presenting respondents with carefully selected and ordered questions is the only practical way to elicit the data required to confirm or disconfirm a hypothesis or to collect information in the absence of a hypothesis. For example, it may be hypothesized that the majority of grammar school teachers are opposed to comprehensive education. One way of obtaining their views would be by means of a questionnaire. Most readers have probably been asked to complete a questionnaire at some time in their lives and will be familiar with the technique. Examples of the use made of questionnaires for research purposes are to be found in the research journals, and include studies by Morrison (1967) in respect of children's attitudes to international affairs, and Johnson (1966) in respect of teachers' attitudes to educational research.

A second research instrument frequently used in descriptive research studies is the interview. It has been found that many persons are more willing to communicate orally than in writing and will therefore provide data more readily and fully in an interview than by completing a questionnaire. Other advantages in the use of an interview will be more fully dealt with in a subsequent chapter; here we merely state that one distinct advantage to be gained by its use in educational research is that it is a particularly useful way of gathering information from children.

In addition to questionnaires and interviews, descriptive studies employ appraisal instruments of various kinds including standardized tests, inventories, scales and sociometric and projective techniques. These and others are frequently made use of in order to gather research information, and they too are also more fully dealt with in chapters 5, 6, and 7.

A further misconception is that the data obtained in descriptive research can only be expressed in qualitative or verbal terms. This is not the case. The term 'descriptive' does not necessarily imply the use of verbal symbols to describe the data which have been collected. Descriptive data may also be expressed in mathematical or quantitative terms. Some research reports may consist exclusively of one form or the other, although most reports make use of both forms. The data obtained in some studies may best be expressed in predominantly qualitative terms; that is to say, the data may be presented in the form of verbal description. Indeed, many pioneering studies in the behavioural sciences in general, and in education in particular, were often expressed in this manner (see Gesell 1955).

Qualitative symbols, however, often lack precision and do not necessarily convey the same meaning to different people. For instance, the level of reading attainment in a particular school may be described as 'poor', or 'fair', or 'very good', but the interpretation put upon these terms by different individuals is likely to vary because of the lack of precision of the qualitative terms used. For this reason, increasing use is being made of quantitative or numerical symbols which have the advantage of conveying information more precisely and are thus less open to misinterpretation. These symbols may be the products of counting or measuring. Thus research workers may count the occurrence or non-occurrence of units, items or categories; for example, the number of children attending a particular school may be expressed in this way. Sometimes, however, the investigator may be more concerned to measure amounts rather than to count items, for example the amount of training required to learn a particular skill, or the level of intelligence of a child may be measured rather than counted.

Types of descriptive research

There is some difficulty in classifying studies which are descriptive in character, but for present purposes they will be considered in the following categories:

1. Survey studies
2. Case studies
3. Developmental studies

SURVEY STUDIES

The survey method is one of the most commonly used methods of descriptive research in the behavioural sciences. It gathers data from a relatively large number of cases at a particular time and is not concerned with the characteristics of individuals as individuals. It is concerned with the generalized statistics that result when data are abstracted from a number of individual cases. A survey is a form of planned collection of data for the purposes of description. It may be broad or narrow in scope, encompassing several countries or be confined to only one nation, local education authority or school. Data may be obtained from a total population or from a representative sample from which generalizations may be made. In analysing political, social or economic conditions one of the first steps is to obtain facts about the existing state of events, and the survey method is frequently employed to achieve this end.

Surveys have been widely used in educational research for many years, and continue to be used to gather information about prevailing conditions. Facts have been gathered through the use of questionnaires, interviews, standardized tests, and other data-gathering techniques, and the analysis of such information has enabled decisions to be made which have transformed many administrative, financial and other practices in the British educational system.

It has long been the practice of the Department of Education and Science and other government agencies to gather information routinely about many aspects of education, and the results can be seen in *Statistics of Education* published annually by the Department of Education and Science. The gathering of facts in this way is not research at a high level—its main purpose is to provide the authorities with information which will form the basis of administrative action. Nevertheless, the data can be used as a basis for further research.

Surveys carried out at the national level by government departments are extremely large and present considerable organizational problems. Most surveys carried out for research purposes are smaller and much less comprehensive, the size depending to some extent upon the resources available. Research foundations such as the National Foundation for Educational Research, and government agencies are often in a position to conduct quite large surveys; e.g. the Plowden Committee (1967) made use of such agencies.* On the other hand, individuals inevitably carry out surveys on a smaller scale.

It is increasingly the practice for surveys to be carried out at the regional level by local education authorities. Educational psychologists employed by many local education authorities investigate the level of attainment in the basic subjects by means of a survey, with a view to determining the incidence of, say, backwardness. Whilst only a few of the results of surveys carried out by local

* See also *Schools Council Enquiry* 1 carried out by the Government Social Survey amoung young school leavers.

authorities have been published, many articles can be found in the journals which demonstrate the use made of the survey method by individuals engaged in research (see Chazan 1964, King 1965, and Lawson and Hartley 1967). It is sometimes argued that some descriptive studies are not research in a precise sense, because very often the information is gathered in a routine manner and is not in the first place sought to demonstrate the worth of a hypothesis erected prior to the work being carried out. This may be so; nevertheless, studies of this nature must be included under the heading of research, because valuable information is collected which may lead to adminstrative action or to later research.

Data sought in surveys

Many different types of educational phenomena can be investigated by means of the survey. These include (1) the conditions under which learning takes place; (2) the characteristics of the educators; and (3) the characteristics of the pupils.

1. *The conditions under which learning takes place*. Surveys may be concerned with the legal, administrative, social and physical factors which influence the educative process. Information may be sought on national and local regulations, recommendations and decisions, as well as on administrative and financial matters. The material or physical conditions of the educational institutions, and the facilities and supplies, may also be investigated. Aspects of the curriculum, and the teaching methods used may be studied together with the results achieved.

2. *The characteristics of educators*. Questions may be asked about the personnel engaged in education, whether they are administrators or teachers. Information may be sought by means of surveys on their number, age, sex, qualifications, experience, and many other of their characteristics. Their function within the educational system may also be studied.

3. *The characteristics of the pupils.* Many surveys have sought information about the characteristics of pupils; teachers will be familiar with this type of study. The pupil's home background, health, abilities and disabilities, achievement, interests and attitudes have been studied and information has been gathered on his extra-curricular activities and social relationships.

Level of complexity of surveys

Survey studies are mainly of the 'what exists' type; that is to say, they are designed to determine the nature of an existing state of affairs. Whilst they can clearly be considered a method of research in that they accumulate data, there are those who question their scientific status, it being argued that scientific knowledge must consist of an organized body of generalizations that explain events and which permit the prediction of events which have not yet occurred. Whilst the survey does not aspire to develop an organized body of knowledge, it does provide useful information of the existence of events and their relationship, and in this sense may serve as a useful basis for research of an experimental nature, which may later lead to the establishment of some theory. The type of survey which provides information of the existence of events or variables has been called the *frequency-count* type. The more complex form which determines whether a relationship exists between events is referred to as the *relational, analytic* or *interrelation of events* type.

The simplest form of survey is the frequency-count type. The purpose of this form is to determine the frequency of occurrence of a particular event. For example, this form of survey could be used to discover the number of special schools or special classes which have been established in a given local education authority. Educators are always in need of the data gathered by this means—they are always in need of simple facts which illustrate a particular situation.

The second type of survey is more complex, and, as already indicated, is known variously as the relational, analytic or the interrelation of events type. This form allows not only for the existence of events to be determined, but also whether a relationship exists between them and the size or magnitude of the relationship. As an example of this type of study let us suppose that we wish to discover whether a relationship exists, and how much of a relationship exists, between level of measured intelligence and attainment in mathematics. As a result of previous experience we may erect the hypothesis that the higher the level of measured intelligence the higher the level of attainment in mathematics. In order to test this hypothesis the following procedure could be followed, which would involve carrying out a survey of the interrelation of events type.

Standardized tests of intelligence and mathematics appropriate for the age group under investigation would require to be administered and the results obtained. By the use of appropriate statistical techniques the two sets of results could then be correlated in order to discover the magnitude or intensity of the relationship between the two variables. The statistical analysis of the results in this way will enable the research worker to discover whether the variables are closely related, moderately related, or completely unrelated. Further, by discovering the intensity of the relationship he will be able to make predictions in relation to future performance on tests of intelligence and mathematics.

Studies of this type can be found in the journals, examples being Douglas, Ross and Cooper (1967), Pidgeon (1965) and Thackray (1965). The Plowden Report (1967) includes more complex examples of this type of study, one of which is described in chapter 9 of this book.

Steps in the construction of a survey

It has been stated previously that surveys should not be undertaken without some purpose and without careful planning. In order to gain the maximum amount of value from a survey the following procedure ought to be adopted in the construction and execution of a survey carried out for the purposes of research.

1. The particular problem of education which is to be investigated has to be identified and clearly stated. This is best done by those who are aware of the problems of educational practice.
2. This step must be followed by a consideration of research previously carried out to investigate the problem, in order to put the investigator into a position in which he can elaborate a hypothesis which is to be tested.
3. Consideration must then be given to the design of the survey and the procedure to be followed in its execution. At this point the nature of the sample to be studied must also be determined.
4. If research instruments are to be used, they must be specified and the advantages and disadvantages of their use in the study discussed. If original research instruments have been devised, detailed information must be furnished on their construction and, if applicable, their standardization.
5. A pilot study is the next step, especially if a research instrument has been constructed. A pilot study is also particularly useful for the training of personnel who may assist in the carrying out of the survey.
6. In carrying out the survey the specified procedures must be closely adhered to; otherwise the results will be invalidated.
7. The results must be reported in terms which are precise and unequivocal. Whether qualitative or quantitative terms are used will depend upon the nature of the results and the expertise of the research worker.
8. The final and important step is the interpretation of the results in the light of previous research and the drawing of

conclusions. This demands a high level of skill and the worth of the study very much depends upon the ability of the research worker to carry out this task effectively.

Advantages and limitations of surveys

The survey method has the advantage of being an extremely effective way of gathering information from a large number of sources, relatively cheaply and in a relatively short time. The results can normally be analysed quickly, allowing action to be taken to effect change if this is indicated and desired. There are limitations, however, especially if information is sought from human beings which is either unknown to them or which they are unwilling to divulge. Furthermore, surveys in themselves do not reveal forecasts of things to come, but they may provide the basis from which predictions can be made using other methods of research.

The survey is an extremely important and widely used type of research, but to be used effectively it entails more than the mere collection of information. A clearly defined problem, a definite purpose and careful planning as well as the skilful analysis and interpretation of the results are required if the aims of the study are to be achieved. The survey method has thus a valuable role to play as a means of providing the educator with an accurate description of some of the variables involved in education.

THE CASE STUDY

The purpose of a *case study* is to examine the characteristics not of a large sample or a total population, but of an individual unit. This unit may be a person, a family, a group, or a community, and the intention is to study the unit at great depth or intensity with a view to establishing generalizations about a wider population of units. The study of a single unit in this way may be thought to be of limited value in establishing generalizations, but there are often distinct advantages in this type of research, especially if the units are representative of a larger population and if the case study is supplemented by other types of research.

It is an extremely widely used method of research in the behavioural sciences, and examples of its use can be found in sociology, psychology, anthropology and education. Case studies have been made of individual children, and of all types of groups in education from the small group within a class to the school itself. Social groups have also been studied; these have varied in size from small groups whose individuals share certain characteristics in common, such as juvenile delinquents and drug addicts, to entire tribes.

Teachers are probably most familiar with studies of individual children, for many of them have undertaken such studies themselves either during initial training or subsequently whilst pursuing courses of advanced study. They are probably familiar with the sort of information which is gathered on home background, intellectual abilities and disabilities, scholastic attainment, attitudes and interests, and relationships with adults and with other children. Careful observation of the child is also undertaken and standardized tests may be given. Studies of this kind are chiefly carried out for training purposes and serve as a means of directing the student's attention towards the behaviour of children. Whilst it is true that they possess only limited research value since they rarely extend present knowledge, they provide the student with training in elementary research techniques and expose him to the difficulties inherent in research work.

Case studies of individuals carried out by professionally qualified persons or by post-graduate research workers are of two types. The *clinical* type of case study is usually carried out by psychiatrists, psychologists and social workers in order to diagnose a particular condition with a view to recommending therapeutic measures. The individual is studied as a unique personality rather than as a representative type and usually the primary object of the study is not research. Only occasionally are the results of such studies published in journals. This does not mean that the information on human behaviour gained in this way is never made available and is not valuable, for research purposes. On the contrary. Freud was primarily concerned with diagnosing and treating the problems of his patients, but his brilliant observation of their behaviour and his interpretation of the causes of that behaviour, led him to derive theoretical formulations which might be applicable to human behaviour in general.

The difficulty posed by research of this kind is that the data gleaned in this way can rarely be checked by other research workers because it has been obtained in a confidential interview. Records of such interviews are sometimes made available with the permission of the persons involved, and they reveal the depth with which the subject has been investigated. It is clear that few other methods of research delve as deeply or produce such a detailed exposure of the psychological state of human beings.

There are other weaknesses in this approach for research purposes. The investigator is usually a clinician oriented towards understanding his patient with a view to helping him rather than with research as his objective. Furthermore, he may be unaware of research methods and techniques and of the safeguards which must be adopted. In the interview situation, however, he is not always in a position to conform to any predetermined plan or set procedure; indeed, the patient rather than the clinician often determines the direction the interview takes. Perhaps the most important weakness, as has been previously suggested, is the confidential nature of the interview and the unavailability of the data to other research workers who may wish to replicate the situation.

The second type of case study used in research is sometimes referred to as the *biographical* type. In this type an account of the individual is provided by means of prolonged study and numerous observations which may spread over years. They are thus longitudinal in character and show changes in the subject with the passage of time and with variation in environment. Whole life spans are rarely studied, and the study is usually confined to some part of life. A good example is Stott's (1961) study of his son's behaviour during the first eighteen months of life.

Early studies of this type were almost always the reports of intelligent parents of their own or their friends' children. They were often carried out unsystematically by persons completely untrained in research techniques; thus the reports were highly selective in the data which was included, and much of the material is anecdotal and collected by hindsight. Studies undertaken today must be carefully planned and the observer's own views supported by as much objective evidence as possible from the use of films, tape recordings, diaries, written records, school books, and the results obtained by the use of appraisal techniques such as standardized tests. The sophisticated procedures adopted by Gesell (1955) in his study of young children provides a good example of the thorough way in which case studies can and ought to be carried out. Biographical studies also need to be undertaken by persons trained in research methods, especially if the purpose is to provide results which will lead to further research.

Advantages and limitations of case studies

The study of individual cases offers many advantages, but there are also limitations in this approach. Studies carried out at great depth by trained and experienced persons may reveal data in a way provided by no other form of research. It is also an extremely useful method to use to study rare or unusual cases of human behaviour, being especially valuable in the study of handicapped subjects and those suffering from rare physical conditions. Berg's (1961) study of a case of congenital auditory imperception provides an illustration of the latter type of study. One final advantage is that the case study method enables a view to be taken of the human being as a unique individual.

The most obvious shortcoming of this method of research is that the cases selected for study may not be representative or typical, and that generalizations made about human behaviour on this basis will not be valid. Indeed, there is a distinct possibility that the unusual or abnormal subject will attract attention and be selected for study. A further limitation is that the interests of the research worker may determine which aspects of behaviour are studied, although this, of course, also applies in other types of research. A final disadvantage is that research based upon the study of a single case or a few cases is extremely expensive in terms of time and financial cost, and it may only be justifiable in relation to cases which are unusual or exceptional.

From case studies information may be obtained which can be gathered by no other means, and which may serve as a basis for further research or be considered in conjunction with information gathered by other methods.

DEVELOPMENTAL STUDIES

The third main type of descriptive research method is the developmental study. Such studies are concerned not only with the present status and interrelation of the variables in a situation, but also with changes which occur as a function of time. In studies of this type investigators describe variables in the course of their development over a period of months or even years. Essentially, recorded data are considered with a view to determining what has happened in the past and what is happening now, either for its own sake or with a view to predicting what is likely to happen in the future.

Educators are inevitably concerned with the physical and mental development of children, and with the changes which take place as a result of the presence or absence of interrelated factors, for education is concerned with change and growth as it occurs in the pupil over a period of time. Child development may be studied by both experimental and descriptive means, but the emphasis in most of the studies has been on the descriptive approach. This was especially true of many of the pioneering studies of child development.

There are two main ways in which child development may be studied: the *longitudinal* and the *cross-sectional* approaches. In longitudinal studies, the same children are studied at intervals during a period of their life span. If the object of the study is to determine the changes which occurred during the period of school attendance, it would be possible to study children at, say, yearly intervals and to plot the patterns of development for each child and for the group as a whole. An alternative way of carrying out such a study would be to study groups of different children at each age level, and to plot the patterns of development—this is the cross-sectional method of studying development over a period of time.

Longitudinal studies are the more effective method of studying development over a period of time, but the bulk of research is cross-sectional in character, chiefly because it is less expensive and time consuming. No length of time is laid down for a longitudinal study; this is determined by the organizers of the project. In certain American studies contact with subjects was initially established as long ago as the 1920s, and some of these studies were maintained for thirty-five years (see Terman and Oden 1959).

Contact with the same group of subjects over a long period offers certain advantages but also poses considerable problems. If the sample chosen is a representative one, the typical pattern of development is revealed, and factors operating on the original sample become apparent which would not normally be revealed in any other way. For example, the effect of death is made apparent especially if the study covers the total life span, since persons who live into adulthood may possess different characteristics from those who do not, and this may be especially true of those who live to a great age.

The longitudinal approach also imposes many difficulties, especially in relation to the collection of the data. The inevitable magnitude of a project which seeks to follow a group of subjects over a number of years demands considerable expenditure in terms of time, money and staff. Such projects also require a considerable amount of planning and farsightedness, with a degree of flexibility built into the design to allow for changes to be made in the future. There are difficulties, too, in relation to the sample of subjects selected for study. It has been known for many years that parents from the middle socio-economic group are more willing to participate, and maintain their interest, in longitudinal studies than parents from the lowest socio-economic group. This poses problems in the selection of a representative sample. On the other hand, parents in the middle-class group have been found to be more mobilet han parents in the lowest group and they are more likely to leave the area in which the study is taking place, thus making it difficult for contact to be retained with their children.

The loss of subjects in this and other ways poses many difficulties. There is the problem of retaining the interest of the subjects over long periods of time. The experience of research workers suggests that this is not too difficult to do whilst the child is attending an educational institution, but the difficulties increase once employment has commenced. Loss of numbers through death is usually small, but if a group is to be studied over a number of years some loss due to migration and other causes is inevitable. One estimate suggests that over a period of ten years only one-third of a group will remain available in the immediate locality in which they were living at the commencement of the period of study. This poses problems, and allowances have to be made in the design to compensate for the inevitable loss of subjects. A final point to do with the subjects involved in longitudinal studies is that their behaviour may be affected by reason of the participation in the research and in consequence their pattern of development may be atypical.

There are difficulties also in relation to the research personnel. Whilst some research projects have been directed by the same person for many years, changes in personnel may affect the continuity of the project, or it may mean a change in emphasis or even in direction.

Clearly some of the organizational difficulties inherent in the design of longitudinal studies do not obtain in cross-sectional studies, and it is the case that most research on human development is cross-sectional in character. The chief advantages of the cross-sectional approach lie in its relative cheapness and the speed with which patterns of development may be obtained. It is much less time consuming than longitudinal research, and it allows for the study to be completed in a relatively short time without a period of years elapsing before the results are known. The chief limitation of this approach, especially if the study is confined to one geographical area, is that it presents difficulties in relation to the selection of age group samples which are representative of the total population. If, for example, the study sought to determine patterns of development between five and eighteen years of age and was confined to one town or county, the samples of older subjects would not include those who had left the area, e.g. to attend educational institutions elsewhere. Consequently generalizations about development based upon the samples of older subjects may not be applicable to young people in general.

Conclusion

Descriptive research is concerned with the observation and description of the factors which exist in a given situation. However, in addition to description it is concerned with the analysis and the interpretation of what is described. Descriptive research may be used to identify objectives and to point to the way in which they may be reached. It is still the most widely used method in educational research and there is a continuing need in education for the collection of information and for descriptions of human behaviour. However, descriptive research does not in itself provide theories which explain why events occur, but it might well provide the data from which theories may be elaborated and so aid the research worker to achieve the aims of behavioural science, namely to explain, control and predict behaviour. It is, however, only by means of experimental research that knowledge is acquired through the direct manipulation of variables, and it is to a consideration of the role of experimental research that we turn in the next chapter.

CHAPTER 4

Experimental research

Many of the investigations carried out in the field of educational research are *ex post facto* studies. They involve the systematic recording of data and its later analysis. These are very important pieces of research, for they result in evidence which, in turn, may well lead to testable hypotheses, generalizations and predictions. But in *experimental research*—in the sense that the natural scientists use the term—we deliberately control and modify the conditions which determine the event in which we are interested; that is to say, it involves the observation and analysis of what happens under carefully controlled conditions. It has been applied with varied success in the educational setting, where, within certain limits, it is sometimes possible to control significant influences to an extent.

Stages in experimental research

The research worker has to work through a number of steps before he can proceed to his main experiment in much the same way as he had to follow certain procedures in descriptive research. Indeed, he has to work through a kind of drill which may be likened to the 'cockpit drill' of the airline pilot. As this book is intended to help readers to interpret research and not in the first instance to help them to inaugurate it, we shall discuss these steps but briefly. In examining reported research, however, readers should see to what extent it appears that investigators did pay attention to the points indicated.

Some problem, amenable to experimental research, has first to be found and analysed. Such a problem may arise out of personal experience, reading, a 'hunch' or discussion with others. The investigator may feel, for example, that children who are taught by method A have a better understanding of electromagnetism than pupils taught by method B. He must then read the relevant literature in order to find out what is known about the topic, redefine his problem if necessary, and trim it to become of manageable size. What this size is depends upon the number, skill and experience of the research team, the financial and other resources available, and the time which would be required. A hypothesis or hypotheses must be clearly and unambiguously formulated and the consequences which follow deduced. In our example it might be that there is no difference in the levels of understanding of electromagnetism due to differences in methods—the null hypothesis (see chapter 8).

Serious attention must then be paid to the points outlined below; indeed, if such attention is not paid, the whole study may turn out to be valueless.

1. The investigator must first decide which variables are likely to affect the knowledge and understanding of pupils in respect of electromagnetism, and which of these he is going to manipulate directly. He may decide, as we suggested above, that it is only the teaching method. Or he may decide that it is both the method and the level of measured intelligence which are the crucial variables.
2. Other variables can then be regarded as non-experimental and the investigator has to decide how he can control for these. He is thus led to consider the general design of his experiment. All that need be said at this point is that if he decides that only the method is an important variable, then the experimental design must ensure that if, say, method A is given to one group of children and method B to a similar group, any differences found in the group scores are due to methods and to no other variable.

3. At the same time as the investigator considers the design for the experiment he must consider the population he is going to work with. For example, is the experiment to deal with pupils of average and superior ability in comprehensive schools, or with pupils of all levels of ability? Or is the experiment to be confined to pupils of one sex?
4. Having decided on the answers to the above and related questions, the investigator must decide on how to get representative samples of the chosen population, how these subjects are to be placed in groups, and how the methods, say, are to be assigned to the groups.
5. A decision must then be reached on the tests, examinations, or other instruments to be used to assess the results of the experiment. Sometimes adequate tools are available; on other occasions new tests have to be devised, as was indicated in the previous chapter. Care must be taken to ensure that the tests are valid ones for estimating the outcome of the research. In the case of different methods being used the tests must be such that they are equally fair to both methods. A test of traditional mathematics may not be equally fair to pupils who have studied ideas introduced into school mathematics in more recent years.
6. To make sure that the experimental procedures will work it is often necessary to have a pilot experiment with small numbers of children.
7. Finally, the null hypothesis must be stated. In our example it would be 'There will be no significant difference in the degree of understanding of electromagnetism resulting from the two different methods'. On analysing the results it may, of course, be found that the hypothesis may be rejected at the 1 per cent or 5 per cent level. It will be recalled that hypotheses are established or rejected in terms of some degree of probability.

Hypothesis testing

It is important to realize in education, as in any other field of inquiry, that although the research worker has found empirical evidence which supports the consequences of a hypothesis, this does not prove that he has found the real cause of some phenomenon. Consider the following instance. It could be hypothesized that young children who experience unsatisfactory relationships with others within the home become delinquent. A consequence of this would be that a disproportionate number of such children would later be found to be delinquent. On investigation it might be found that among the majority of delinquents there were these conditions of unsatisfactory relationships within the home during the early years. Nevertheless, one could not, on this evidence alone, say that the unsatisfactory conditions within the home are the *cause* of delinquency. It could be that unsatisfactory home relationships and delinquency are certainly *associated* with one another, but other factors could also be associated with delinquency. It is not until the experimenter has eliminated other possible explanations that he can claim that his hypothesis is the only one adequate to explain the phenomenon. Naturally if much factual evidence is found which supports several of the deductions from a given hypothesis, the degree of probability of that hypothesis offering a satisfactory explanation increases.

Although a hypothesis may offer the best explanation of some phenomenon and even be regarded as 'cast iron', it may have to be modified or even abandoned when fresh facts are discovered which are inconsistent with the deduced consequences of it. A further point to note is that hypotheses should not be necessarily rejected if one is unable to obtain evidence consistent with the deduced consequences, providing the facts obtained are not inconsistent with the deductions. It may be that evidence is hard to find at the moment although the hypothesis is a good one.

Dependent and independent variables

We have throughout stressed the importance of elaborating a hypothesis and deducing the consequences that should follow from it. If this is done in a satisfactory manner, it will become apparent that there are two factors that will be precisely identified. These are an independent variable (say, the method) and the dependent variable (say, the response). More generally the former may be looked upon as condition A which causes condition B—the dependent variable. Thus in experimental research the investigator devises an experiment in which he does his best to control all conditions other than the independent variable, which he deliberately manipulates. At the same time he observes what happens to the dependent variable. It is clear that when the research worker has identified and controlled all the factors that influence the dependent variable, he can be sure that it is the independent variable that has caused the changes in the dependent variable. The investigator may, of course, wish to manipulate two independent variables. Indeed, it is sometimes important to do this. For example, in our example both the measured intelligence of the pupils and the teaching method may be regarded as dependent variables which determine the understanding of electromagnetism. Moreover, these two as independent variables may, acting together, bring new knowledge if there was an important interaction effect between them: for example, certain levels of measured intelligence might interact with a particular method to bring about increased understanding.

Experimental controls

The first task of the investigator is to determine which variables affect his dependent variable. Here his own experience in the field is likely to be of some help, but probably of greater importance (unless he is very experienced) are the findings of other research workers and the clues they give in related research already published. Control must be then exercised over these variables—

other than those regarded as independent ones in the experiment—for three reasons. First, we have to remove or hold constant the unwanted variables so that we can isolate the independent variable or variables which interest us. If in our example we wish to isolate the possible effects of previous knowledge on the understanding of electromagnetism so that we can test for the effects of teaching method, then in one way or another the variable of previous knowledge must be equalized in the groups of children receiving the different teaching methods. Second, the experimental conditions must be controlled so that it will be possible to study changes in the magnitude of the independent variable and the corresponding effects on the dependent variable. It is sometimes the case that the independent variable affects the dependent variable within certain limits only. For example, I.Q. may be related to the class of university degree up to an I.Q. of, say, 115; after that, I.Q. may be a relatively unimportant variable. Last, the conditions of the experiment must be controlled in the hope that it will be possible both to determine the precise degree of relationship between the variables and to express the relationship in numerical terms.

It has been pointed out that the methods used in controlling variables can be put into three broad categories (Brown and Geselli 1955). In educational research the most frequently used method is that of the selective manipulation of variables. In this the pupils are selected in such a way that the research worker obtains control over many unwanted variables such as age, measured intelligence, sex and social background. Or the groups of pupils may receive their 'treatment' (whatever that may be) always in the same classroom or at the same time of day. Again, the materials used in the teaching and the exercises to be worked may be made comparable in difficulty as far as possible. In these and other ways we selectively manipulate the variables we want out of the way, in order to assess the influence of the variable or variables in which we are interested.

A second method often used in educational research is known as the statistical manipulation of the variables. Suppose that variables W, X and Y act together on the dependent variable Z. If we study only the relationship between changes in W and changes in Z, our results will be spurious. A statistical technique is needed which will enable us to hold constant the effects of X and Y while we determine the precise effects of W on Z. For example, suppose that age, scholastic attainment and attitude are three variables affecting the dependent variable Z, then it is possible, using such a technique, to find the effects of each in turn. Occasionally partial correlation can be used to do this, but more often we use a technique known as *analysis of variance*. The third method used in controlling variables—physical manipulation—is but rarely used in educational research, although it is more often used in more general psychological research. In this method the physical conditions of the experimental situation are controlled so that, for example, pupils are all exposed to the same stimuli (say, words) for an equally short length of time, or the conditions controlled so that all unwanted auditory stimuli (say) are eliminated.

Some further problems in educational research

It may be decided to introduce, say, a topic in history to one group of children by using a new approach, while another group of pupils are introduced to the topic by a more traditional method. Or one group may have extra time devoted to spelling and another group may have the normal amount of time devoted to it. In each instance the first may be called the *experimental* and the second the *control* group. We are, of course, interested in the attainment and understanding of the pupils after they have been subjected to different 'treatments'. Indeed, in these examples the attainment or understanding would be the dependent variable.

Now it has already been stressed that the groups which receive different 'treatments' must be made equivalent in respect of all the factors that may influence the dependent variable except for the factor or factors that we chose as independent variables. The best way to do this is to allocate pupils to the experimental and control groups by drawing random names from a hat or by the use of a table of random numbers. By using a random procedure we are most likely to render the two groups equivalent from the point of view of I.Q., age, previous experience, etc. The larger the groups the truer this is likely to be. Conversely, in the case of small groups, there is a greater possibility that differences in the groups will occur, so there is a greater tendency for, say, the taller or the more intelligent to be found in one of the groups. It must also be recognized that when the effects of the independent variable are small, these may be masked by differences in the original composition of the experimental and control groups even when care has been taken over random assignment to the groups.

Matching techniques

On occasions matching techniques are employed. In the *matched pair technique*, pairs of subjects who are as alike as possible in respect of, say, age, measured intelligence, attainment, or other variable, are selected and members of each pair allocated at random to each of the two 'treatments'. Exact matching on more than three variables is unlikely, and it is often difficult to match even on two. Naturally some of the pairs may drop out during the course of the experiment and in this case the matching design may be impaired. Another difficulty which may arise is due to what is known as 'regression towards the mean'. This will be explained later in the chapter.

Much use has also been made of *matched groups*. In this, experimental and control groups are selected so that they have roughly the same mean and approximately the same standard deviation in respect of some variable or variables. Yet difficulties may arise. Suppose that the groups have been matched on two variables *P* and Q. Although the means and standard deviations of *P* and Q for the two groups are the same,* it is still possible for the two groups to have different combinations of these variables. For example, the members of the experimental group could have a low *P* and high Q, and high *P* and low Q, whereas members of the control group could have high *P* and high Q, and low *P* and low Q. Such differences could affect the result of the research in spite of the fact that the groups were matched in terms of the means and standard deviations.

It is clear from what has been said that pupils should, ideally, be randomly assigned to different treatments. Sometimes, however, this is not possible. Classes of pupils have often to be taken as they are found. For example, we may have to accept one group of pupils taking GCE 'A' level History and another within the same form which is not, and matching pairs of pupils in respect of age, I.Q., attainments, etc., may be very difficult. Fortunately, a statistical technique known as *analysis of covariance* enables the experimenter to adjust the final scores or assessments made after the treatments, to make allowance for the lack of equivalence found between the experimental and control groups at the beginning of the study. So, while matching is occasionally necessary, analysis of covariance can generally achieve the same results with much less difficulty.

Simple experimental designs

In this section we discuss a few simple experimental designs; ones used in actual research are often more complex. But those discussed here will give readers some insight into a few of the problems that have to be faced in rigorous experimental research.

The first design involves the selection of subjects from the

* It will be appreciated that the mean and standard deviation of *P* need not equal those of Q. It is between groups that the corresponding means and standard deviations must be equal.

general population by random methods if this is at all possible. Whether or not it is possible, subjects should be assigned to the different treatment groups using random methods. Suppose, for example, that we wish to test the effectiveness of a new approach to the teaching of spelling to eight-year-olds against a more traditional approach to the topic. The group which acts as the control is, in this instance, the one which undergoes the traditional approach. We should begin by selecting a sample from some wider population of eight-year-olds and then allocate the members of the sample to the groups experiencing the new approach (T_1) and the traditional method (T_2) by random procedures. A pre-test is given followed by the required period of teaching, at the same time making sure as far as possible that all other conditions remain the same for the two groups. Finally a post-test of spelling would be given, the test being equally fair to both groups.

We now have sufficient data to tell us whether the difference between the differences in the post-test scores and pre-test scores is statistically significant. Let the mean pre-test scores for the experimental and control groups be m_1 and m_2 respectively, and the mean post-test scores be M_1 and M_2, with the latter being adjusted for pre-test differences if the technique of analysis of covariance is being employed. Otherwise the differences $M_1 - m_1 = D_1$ and $M_2 - m_2 = D_2$ are calculated, and a test applied to determine if the difference $D_1 - D_2$ is statistically significant. Expressed in table form we have:

Group	*Pre-test mean*	*Treatment*	*Post-test mean*
Experimental	m_1	T_1	M_1
Control	m_2	T_2	M_2

It is, of course, quite feasible to compare the performance of two or more experimental groups with that of the control group. In that instance we might be investigating, say, two new approaches to a topic and comparing their effectiveness both one with another and with that of a more traditional approach. In this case the table would be:

Group	*Pre-test mean*	*Treatment*	*Post-test mean*
Experimental 1	m_1	T_1	M_1
Experimental 2	m_2	T_2	M_2
Control	m_3	T_3	M_3

Although this general type of design overcomes some difficulties, others remain. For example, if three different teachers take the three methods, then teacher effectiveness or teacher personality may affect the post-test scores rather than method effectiveness. On the other hand, if one teacher takes all three methods he may show more competence in, or enthusiasm for, one method rather than for the other two. Again, it may be impossible to generalize the findings obtained from one school to all schools across the country. Indeed, unless samples are large and representative of the whole population, extreme care must be taken over the generalization of the results. Finally, there may be an interaction between pre-testing and treatment. The members of one of the groups may become very interested in spelling as a result of the pre-test and may work hard and show enthusiasm for it, regardless of method. In this case the results will be invalid, since they result from such interaction and not from method *per se*. Naturally, if pre-test scores are available in the form of normal class test results, then no specific pre-testing programme is necessary and the design is adequate in this respect.

If a large sample of pupils is available, or the pre-testing is liable to interact with the treatment, or the anonymity of the subjects has to be maintained (as when pupils give a better performance if their names are not on the answer sheets), the following design may be used:

Group	*Pre-test mean*	*Treatment*	*Post-test mean*
Experimental	–	T	M_1
Control	–	–	M_2

In other words, no pre-test is given, but the sample is reckoned to be large enough for it to be assumed that the two groups are equated in respect of the dependent and other variables. However, the first design discussed should be used if possible. Indeed, if it is suspected that there is an interaction between pre-testing and treatment, the first design can be modified to give two further groups, one an experimental and one a control group. Pupils would, of course, be randomly assigned to the four groups. In this case one would have:

Group	*Pre-test mean*	*Treatment*	*Post-test mean*
Experimental 1	m_1	T	M_1
Control 1	m_2	–	M_2
Experimental 2	–	T	M_3
Control 2	–	–	M_4

To find the effect of the treatment alone the difference $M_3 - M_4$ is calculated; while to establish the extent of the interaction effect on its own we calculate $(M_1 - m_1) - (M_2 - m_2) - M_3$.

The research worker might well like to work with the kinds of design that have just been discussed. But, as was mentioned earlier, he has often in practice to work with intact classes as he finds them. The experimental design is then much the same as our first one, but the subjects have not been randomly assigned to the groups. Thus one would have:

Group	*Pre-test mean*	*Treatment*	*Post-test mean*
Experimental	m_1	T	M_1
Control	m_2		M_2

However, there clearly remains the danger that although the mean pre-test scores for the two groups may be almost the same, the groups may yet differ in a number of ways. For example, consider the case where the experimental group is taking History in the GCE 'A' level examinations but the control group is not. Although the members of the two groups may be matched for age, sex, I.Q. and some aspect of school attainment, it would be more than likely that the school experience of the two groups would differ and that the groups might diverge in their knowledge of, and attitudes to, certain topics happening currently. It is, therefore, very difficult at times to know if the differences eventually found between the groups is due to the treatment or to other variables.

The above designs, while clearly outlining some of the basic problems facing the investigator, takes into account only one variable at a time. However, very often in education there are two or more variables acting simultaneously and in such cases a more complex design must be used. It was posited earlier in the chapter that both teaching method and level of measured intelligence might be variables affecting the understanding of electromagnetism. To test this a design based on analysis of variance would be used. This may well show that both these independent variables do affect the dependent variable but, just as important, it may also show that there is an interaction between level of intelligence and teaching method, which suggests, for example, that one of the methods is of more value with pupils of lower measured intelligence. These interactions are often of great importance and they cannot be obtained from the simple designs outlined earlier. This is one reason why research now very often employs designs based on analysis of variance, for we can investigate the effects of two or more independent variables acting together and assess the significance of their interactions.

Sometimes it is desired to maintain the treatment over a long period, say a school year, and give a number of tests to both the experimental and control groups at intervals throughout the year. Analysis of variance can determine if both groups improved their performance on successive testings, whether the experimental group's performance on the last testing was better than that of the control group, or whether the rates of improvement for the groups was essentially the same. Readers who are especially interested in the design of experiments should consult an appropriate text.*

Regression to the mean

Readers need to be on their guard in educational research, especially in experimental work, against the effects of what is known in statistics as *regression to the mean*. Consider the situation in which we select candidates with the bottom 5 per cent of scores on a test. If the test is given again, there will obviously be another 5 per cent of candidates at the bottom. However, on account of the test unreliability (no test has a reliability of 1·0) it will not be quite the same set of candidates as was at the bottom of the list of scores on the first testing. The pupils who got the scores comprising the bottom 5 per cent on the first testing will, on the average, tend to get slightly higher scores on the second testing, while some of those pupils who scored just outside on the first testing will now be included in the bottom 5 per cent on the second. Thus the mean of the scores of those candidates comprising the bottom 5 per cent of scores on the first testing will move slightly towards the mean of the parent population on the second testing.

Likewise consider the candidates who obtained the top 5 per cent of scores. When given the test again their scores will tend to be lower, so that the mean of the group will once again have moved towards the population mean. Thus the top 5 per cent of scores on re-testing will not be obtained by quite the same group of pupils. In both instances, then, the mean of the original group 'regressed' towards the mean of the parent population.

It is thus important to note that the mean of extreme groups will move towards the population mean whether or not any

* For example, LEWIS, D. G. (1968) *Experimental Design in Education*. London: University of London Press Ltd.

treatment is given. The fact that the tests are not completely reliable ensures that although a given group of pupils will obtain rather similar scores on the pre- and post-tests, the scores will vary within a range. Furthermore, the more extreme the pupils' scores are in relation to the mean of the parent population, the more likely they are to vary. Thus when research results are reported, especially those which deal with extreme groups, readers must make sure that the effects of statistical regression have been allowed for when appropriate. Otherwise an error of judgement may be made in respect of the amount of the effect of the treatment.

The effects of regression to the mean can also have unfortunate effects when dealing with matched groups. Consider this extreme case. Suppose that two groups each have a mean score of 120 on the test on which they have been matched. But at the same time suppose that one group has been selected from a school or other parent population in which the mean score was 160 on the test, while the second group was selected from a school where the mean score was only 80 on the test. When the groups are retested their means will regress to the means of the parent populations. This differential degree of regression may even have more effect than the treatment. If the treatment had been given to the first group, more will be attributed to the treatment than is warranted, whereas had the treatment been given to the second group, its effects would be underestimated.

CHAPTER 5

Instruments of research 1: introduction and tests

The evaluation of research instruments

At some point in the design of a research project consideration must be given to the collection of data. This collection of data is obviously an important part of the research process and many data-gathering tools or techniques have been developed to aid the investigator in this task. The techniques vary in complexity in respect of their design, administration and interpretation; each is appropriate for the collection of certain kinds of information and the investigator must select the ones which will provide the data he seeks. He may find that existing ones do not suit his purposes, and he may modify them or even construct new ones. A research worker must therefore possess considerable knowledge about the techniques available to him, and he must also know something of their advantages and limitations if he is to select those which will enable him to collect his data.

For present purposes data-gathering techniques may be classified into three types: (1) tests, (2) self-report techniques, and (3) observational techniques.

Tests consist of a series of tasks which the subject is required to perform. They are mainly concerned with the subject's best possible, or maximum performance. Some provide information on mental abilities, either general intellectual ability or special abilities, whilst others are concerned with attainment or achievement and are designed to demonstrate the level of knowledge or skill which has been acquired as a result of tuition or training.

Certain kinds of information can only be obtained directly

from the subject by asking him to report on his attitudes or beliefs, on the topics in which he is interested, or on his relationships with other members of the group to which he belongs. Techniques which enable the investigator to obtain information in this way are referred to as self-report techniques and are usually constructed in the form of a questionnaire. Different types of questionnaires have been developed for the collection of specific kinds of information; these include scales and inventories, as well as sociometric and projective techniques.

Information may also be obtained through noting behaviour. The observer can either be non-participating or an interviewer. Various techniques have been devised to aid the investigator in his task; these include the interview, check lists, rating scales, and time sampling, incident sampling and controlled diary techniques.

Tests will be discussed in the remainder of this chapter, self-report techniques in chapter 6 and observational techniques in chapter 7. Before proceeding, however, we must first consider the validity and reliability of those techniques which have been devised to evaluate or measure behaviour, and which have been constructed for use in a standardized way. These include tests, attitude scales and inventories.

VALIDITY

In general a technique is valid if it measures what it claims to measure. Validity is therefore concerned with the extent to which a technique actually measures what it was intended to measure. A technique, however, does not possess universal validity—it may be valid for use in one situation but invalid if used in another. There are different types of validity including (1) content validity, (2) predictive validity, (3) concurrent validity, and (4) construct validity.

Content validity

Content validity, which is also known as 'face validity' or

'validity by assumption', is concerned with the content of the technique. In order to determine content validity the investigator must examine the technique to see what it involves. He must have some idea of those areas which the technique should cover, and must then examine it to see if the items it contains adequately cover or represent the various aspects of the subject or topic which is to be assessed.

Predictive validity

A technique which forecasts the kind of behaviour it was intended to forecast (e.g. performance in a job) is said to possess predictive or empirical validity. Predictive validity thus refers to the association between present results and future behaviour, and in order to determine the predictive validity of a technique the results from it must be compared with actual performance in the future. If a test is designed to select pupils for further education, for example, scores on the test should show a high positive correlation with ultimate success in this field. A problem arises in assessing predictivity, however, in that establishing the criteria to measure an outcome—in the above example this is success in further education—may be difficult because there may be differences of opinion, even amongst experts, as to the criteria of success which are to be selected.

It is worth noting at this point that many so-called tests of intelligence have a high degree of predictive validity in spite of the differences of opinion which exist as to the nature of intelligence. These tests are effective in predicting academic success and they therefore serve a useful purpose.

Concurrent validity

In order to establish concurrent validity, the results obtained by means of using a technique can be compared with other measures of performance made at the same time. These measures may be teachers' ratings, or the results obtained from other techniques which have been validated previously. Concurrent validity is thus concerned with the technique's ability to provide an estimate of present performance. It should be noted, however, that whilst concurrent validity provides immediate evidence of the usefulness of the technique, it does not mean that it necessarily has predictive validity.

Construct validity

Construct validity is more complex than the other types of validity. It is concerned not only with the technique itself but also with the theory which seeks to explain, or to account for the results which are obtained when the technique is used. Construct validity is concerned with the interpretation of the scores obtained in terms of psychological constructs. A construct, it will be remembered, is an ability or other characteristic which is hypothesized to explain certain aspects of behaviour such as intelligence or anxiety.

In the process of construct validation the investigator must begin by examining the technique and then suggest constructs which might account for performance on the technique. He then has to derive hypotheses from the theory he has put forward and test these by carrying out experimental studies.

These four types of validity can be classified under primary or secondary validity. Primary or direct validity depends upon the judgements or opinion of experts who, after examining the content of the technique, decide what they think it measures. Secondary or derived validity involves the comparison or correlation of the results obtained by use of the technique with results obtained by other established techniques. Educators are chiefly interested in two kinds of derived validity, concurrent and predictive validity, which have already been discussed.

The procedure for assessing the content, concurrent, predictive and construct validity of a research technique involves one or more of the following:

1. Inspection of the content of the technique to make judgements about what is being assessed.
2. Correlating the results with some external criterion, which may be teachers' estimates, examination results or performance on a technique which measures the same factor as the technique which is being validated.
3. Using factor analysis in order to discover what is being measured by the instrument.

Information should be given on the reliability (see later in chapter) and validity of all those techniques which are used for research purposes, and on the methods which have been used to determine these.

The validity coefficient

The validity of a technique is reported in terms of the validity coefficient. This is the coefficient of correlation between the technique and the criterion measures which have been used in the validation procedure. A correlation coefficient can, of course, vary from +1·0, which is perfect positive correlation, through 0·0 to −1·0, which is perfect negative correlation. To be of value a technique ought to have a validity of at least +0·7, but many techniques with lower coefficients are used in the absence of better ones, especially if they measure something for which no other technique has been constructed.

RELIABILITY

The ultimate consideration concerning any technique is its validity, the extent to which it measures what it is supposed to measure, but the concurrent and predictive validity of a technique is dependent upon its reliability, i.e. its ability to consistently yield the same results when repeated measurements are taken of the same subjects under the same conditions. If a pupil receives a score of 100 on an intelligence test, for example, he should receive approximately the same score when the test is given on a second occasion.

Repeated measures of an individual's intelligence or mathematical attainment may produce different results. These may be due to either a real change in behaviour, which is always possible, or to the unreliability of the test or instrument which is used. If the variation in results is due to a change in behaviour, the reliability of the test is not in question. The different results can, however, be due to the unreliability of the measuring instrument itself. A technique is said to be unreliable if different scores are obtained when it is given a second time, just as the thermometer would be unreliable if it recorded changes in temperature which had not in fact taken place.

There are several ways of measuring the reliability of a technique—which one is used will depend on the circumstances. Just three are outlined here: (1) *the test-retest*, (2) *the equivalent forms*, and (3) *the split-half methods.*

1. *The test-retest method.* In this method the same instrument is re-administered shortly after the first administration, and the two sets of results are correlated and its reliability obtained. A disadvantage of this method is that if the time interval is short, a false impression of the reliability of the instrument may be given, since some subjects may remember certain responses. On the other hand, if the time interval is long, real changes in behaviour may have taken place.

2. *The equivalent forms method.* This method requires that two equivalent or parallel forms of an instrument are prepared, administered to the same group of subjects and the results compared. Readers may be familiar with the two parallel

forms of the second revision of the Stanford-Binet Intelligence Scale (Terman and Merrill 1937), Forms L and M. To obtain the reliability of the instrument the scores on the parallel forms are correlated. It is difficult to construct two parallel forms of an instrument to measure the same thing, and sometimes the reliability obtained through parallel forms is low. In spite of this, the equivalent forms method of determining reliability is widely used. It is worth noting that practice effects are not eliminated by this method.

3. *The split-half method.* In this method the score on one half of the items of the instrument is compared with the score on the other half. The items may be divided into two groups in a variety of ways. In a test of 100 items, for example, one half may be composed of the odd-numbered items, the other half of the even-numbered ones. Alternatively the first 50 items may be compared with the last 50 items. This method measures the internal reliability of the test and if the two halves do not correlate highly it suggests that they are not measuring the same thing. Furthermore, it has the advantage of controlling the effects of boredom, fatigue and practice. It should be noted, however, that timed tests must be split in terms of time rather than in terms of items.

The reliability coefficient

The usual way of reporting the reliability of a research instrument is by means of the reliability coefficient. This is the coefficient of correlation between the test and retest scores of the same subjects on the same form or on parallel forms of the instrument, or between the scores on the two halves of the instrument. To be of value for prediction purposes, an instrument ought to have a reliability coefficient of at least +0·90 whatever method of assessing reliability is used. Many techniques do not possess this high level of reliability, but they are sometimes used for research purposes in the absence of anything more reliable.

Tests

Tests are widely used in education, psychology and psychiatry, and are amongst the most useful tools of research. They have been designed to measure general intellectual ability, aptitudes, attainment or achievement, personality traits, attitudes and interests. They are widely used for the purpose of selection, classification and guidance as well as for the evaluation of educational and therapeutic programmes.

A test has been variously defined. Cronbach's (1960) definition of a test, for example, is extremely broad, since he includes any systematic procedure which is used to compare the behaviour of two or more persons. In a recent publication, *Psychological Tests: A Statement*, by the British Psychological Society (1966), it was considered desirable 'that the term "test" should be restricted to assessment techniques yielding ratings or scores derived from procedures clearly described in the test manual, and based on adequate standardization data'. This definition would thus exclude any technique which is unstandardized and which involves qualitative assessment and subjective judgement of the data.

It is worth noting at this point that we do not discuss the Piagetian or clinical-type approach to the individual testing of children. This approach has been used by many workers in studying the growth of thinking and of concept formation, and is *of the greatest importance in helping us to understand the intellectual growth of children.* The fields in which this general approach has been used have been so numerous, and the techniques so varied, that it would be impossible to do justice to the approach by attempting a treatment of it in this book. Piaget, Piaget and Inhelder, Beilin, Elkind, Lovell, Lunzer, Wohlwill and many others have made extensive use of the approach, and their books and published papers should be consulted. At the time of writing, in only a few studies has an attempt been made to standardize the tests used. Yet in spite of this, *this approach has done more to show the qualitative differences in children's thinking at different age levels than standardized tests have* (see also the end of chapter 9).

A standardized test is one that has specific directions for administration and scoring, a fixed set of test items, and has been given to representative samples taken from the population for whom the test is intended for the purpose of establishing norms. The standard procedure and content allows for an identical test to be given to individuals in different places and at different times. In consequence an individual's score on a standardized test may be compared with the scores of others who have taken the same test. Norms or standards of normal achievements are usually the average scores made by the representative groups of individuals at different age levels, but they may also be provided in respect of other groups, for example, groups of stated occupations or experience. Norms make it possible to compare an individual's score with other individuals whose characteristics are known. It is thus possible to administer a standardized test to a subject and compare his performance with that of, say, an average ten-year-old or a typical third-year primary school child.

The chief value of standardized tests for research purposes lies in their use as instruments of comparison. The norms or standards of normal achievement offer a criterion against which the performance of subjects may be compared with what is normal and usual for their particular age. This is very useful indeed because an awareness of national standards can be gained, and differences in levels of performance in different regions can be measured. Furthermore, differences in ability and attainment between the sexes might also be discovered, while those who are likely to benefit from particular forms of education (e.g. special) can be identified. Such information serves as a useful basis for administrative planning and it is most economically and efficiently obtained through the use of standardized tests. Standardized tests are as objective as possible: the marking and scoring is objective, unambiguous and simple, and is not open to interpretation by the tester.*

There are, however, certain possible disadvantages in the use of tests. They may possess neither high reliability nor high validity, while their indiscriminate use may lead to the entry of practice effects.

THE CONSTRUCTION OF A TEST

Not all tests are good ones and each must be carefully examined in order to assess its worth. Neither the construction nor the refinement of a test is an easy matter and many considerations have to be kept in mind.

The research worker must first define rather precisely the aspect of behaviour which is to be tested. If no satisfactory tests are available, he must design a test to cover all the required facets. He must decide upon the length of the test and the level of difficulty of the items. Both these factors depend upon the age of the group for which the test is intended. Many more items need to be constructed than will be included in the final test, for only those which prove to be effective should be included in the final version of the test.

The test, or several parallel tests, should then be administered in the form of a pilot study to a sample of subjects with similar characteristics to those for whom the test is intended. Their responses can then be examined in an attempt to reveal: (a) sources of confusion and ambiguity in the instructions and in the items, (b) how well the test as a whole discriminates among the

* Some objective tests do permit open-ended responses to some of the items.

subjects, and (c) the contribution of each item to the total effectiveness of the test. Sources of ambiguity must be corrected and those items which prove unsatisfactory must be replaced, and further pilot studies carried out until a satisfactory version is obtained. The procedures outlined in this paragraph are technically complex and, although some further details are given in chapter 9, it is suggested that readers should refer to, say, Anstey (1966) for a fuller discussion.

The final step is to standardize the test. This would be done by administering the test to a large representative sample of subjects for whom the test is intended. On the basis of the results, norms or standards of normal achievement would be obtained from which an individual's rank in a typical group of subjects may be estimated.

Evidence must then be obtained as to the reliability and validity of the test before it is published. These concepts have been discussed already in relation to measuring instruments in general and will be referred to again when the different types of instruments are considered.

THE ADMINISTRATION OF TESTS

Tests vary in complexity. Some are quite simple and require little training for their successful administration. Others are more complex and may require months of training. In the United Kingdom the National Foundation for Educational Research (1969), which distributes many tests through its Test Agency, divides tests into six levels according to the fields of work in which they are used and the levels of qualification of the prospective test users. All users of tests, whatever the level of complexity of the tests, must become familiar with every aspect of a test before administering it. They must also ensure that they adhere strictly to the procedures which are prescribed in the test manual, and that they give no additional assistance to the subjects.

The establishment of a good relationship between tester and testee is important, but creating this relationship requires a high degree of skill. A cold impersonal manner on the part of the tester or, on the other hand, too friendly an approach, may not achieve the desired rapport.

TYPES OF TEST

Tests may be classified in various ways. A distinction between them may be made in terms of the way in which they are administered. *Group* tests differ from individual tests in that they are designed to be used with many subjects at the same time and with the subjects recording their own answers. *Individual* tests are designed to be used in an interview-type situation in which the examiner asks questions and usually records the subject's replies.

A further distinction can be made between *pencil-and-paper* tests and *performance* tests. The pencil-and-paper test requires the subject to respond by writing his replies, whilst in the performance test, problems are presented in a concrete form and the testee is required to respond not by writing but by manipulating apparatus or cards.

Finally tests can be classified in terms of what they claim to measure. Thus a distinction may be made between tests of *mental ability*, *aptitude* tests, and tests of *attainment* or achievement.

GROUP TESTS

Group tests are used more extensively than individual tests chiefly because of their economy in time and labour. They are particularly useful where large numbers of subjects have to be tested at the same time, for example, army recruits or school children.

Group tests are usually carefully timed, the whole group starting and finishing the test according to the tester's directions. Such tests are usually simple to administer, mark, and score, and are therefore widely used for research purposes. They are best used, however, for screening, that is to say for the initial classification or grading of subjects rather than for obtaining precise information about individuals. Furthermore, they are unlikely to yield reliable results when used with young children, i.e. children below the age of seven years; when used with semi-literate or illiterate subjects, or with subjects who are emotionally disturbed. Thus caution must be exercised in evaluating the findings of research studies in which group tests have been used with samples which contained these kinds of children or adults.

INDIVIDUAL TESTS

Individual tests are most appropriately used where the objective is to obtain a precise and detailed assessment of an individual subject. They are normally administered in a single interview, which permits the tester to observe the subject more closely than in the group interview situation. Group tests can, of course, be given to individuals in an interview situation, but individual tests have been designed for use only with individual subjects and cannot be used as group tests. Some individual tests or parts of them are designed to be orally presented and call for oral replies. Others require additional questions to be put for the purpose of clarification. There are also individual tests which have been devised for use with young children, semi-literate and illiterate subjects, and for those who suffer from some form of physical handicap, e.g. partial hearing loss. Considerable training and experience is required to administer many individual tests, and in evaluating the findings of research studies in which such tests have been used the qualifications and experience of the researchers who have administered the tests must be taken into consideration.

PENCIL-AND-PAPER TESTS

Pencil-and-paper tests pose questions in the form of sentences, or designs, and require the respondent to record his answer either by underlining, ticking or ringing one of the alternative answers which are provided, or by writing a word, phrase or sentence in a blank space provided for the purpose. In verbal pencil-and-paper tests, it is inevitable that some level of reading ability is required in order to be able to understand the instructions, the questions and the answers, and such tests are not suitable for use with illiterate or non-English-speaking subjects.

PERFORMANCE TESTS

Performance tests are usually designed in such a way that the questions are presented in a concrete form and call for the subject to respond by manipulating pieces of apparatus, e.g. wooden blocks or cards. Such tests do not generally lend themselves to group administration and are usually presented to individual subjects.

TESTS OF MENTAL ABILITY

Mental ability has been measured by the use of tests for many years, but there has not been complete agreement as to the precise nature of what is being assessed. The views held, however, do overlap to some extent, and most psychologists would accept a definition which includes the ability to discover relevant relationships and the ability to apply these relationships to new but similar situations. Some of the items in the older tests of mental ability appear to test general knowledge, but many items in modern tests emphasize more the ability to discover relationships.

All these tests measure aspects of what man regards as intelligent behaviour, and all measure something of what has been learnt. However, tests which measure knowledge and skills which have been deliberately taught are called attainment tests, and those which measure the more general qualities of thinking which appear to be acquired without specific tuition, such as reasoning ability, comprehension and level of conceptual development, are referred to as tests of mental ability or intelligence. Thus both attainment and intelligence tests measure past learning or attainment, but intelligence tests are not so directly dependent on this as are attainment tests.

Tests of mental ability have been widely used because scores on them generally correlate more highly than the scores on any other type of test with a child's educational progress as a whole, and because they have often proved to be the best single predictor of future educational performance. Thus, whilst there is some disagreement as to the nature of intelligence and whilst many tests are not perfect measuring instruments, they serve a most useful purpose and are the best means of assessment of mental ability we have at the present time.

Tests of intelligence are similar to attainment tests in construction and scoring. They more usually consist of a battery or number of sub-tests each of which contains a series of items of similar content that are graded in difficulty. In a minority of tests, those which Vernon (1956) has referred to as the 'omnibus' type, items of many different kinds are presented in a continuous flow and are not divided into sub-tests. In the battery type, each sub-test is given separately almost as a test within a test. In the omnibus form, items are presented without pause and this sometimes leads to fatigue.

Tests of mental ability may be classified in various ways, but only group and individual types will be considered here. Group tests of mental ability are mainly used by those who have to deal at any one time with large groups of subjects. They are particularly useful in that they rarely require highly trained testers. They are widely used for selection, guidance and for research purposes. The National Foundation for Educational Research (1968b) publishes many group tests of mental ability, details of which are given in their catalogue, *Educational Guidance in Schools*, and most experienced teachers have used or have helped to administer some of these tests.

Group tests of mental ability may be classified into *verbal* and *non-verbal* types. In both types the child records his or her responses in a booklet provided for the purpose. Verbal tests demand the manipulation of ideas which are expressed in words. The majority of tests employ the verbal medium, since man's thinking and reasoning activities generally involve the use of words, numbers or other symbols; and as school work is itself predominantly verbal, verbal tests have been found to be particularly useful in predicting educational performance. Verbal tests of mental ability generally include the following kinds of items:

1. *Analogies.* The subject has to select a fourth word, which is to a third word as a second word is to a first word.
   e.g. Shoe is to foot as hat is to (face, eyes, arm, *head*).
2. *Synonyms and antonyms.* The subject has to underline the word which is the same or opposite in meaning.
   e.g. Fat (light, slow, *thin*, heavy).
3. *Sentence completion.* An incomplete sentence is given and the subject is required to supply the word or words that best complete it.
   e.g. There are .... weeks in a year.
4. *Classification.* The subject has to underline a given number of words that are alike in some way or that belong together.
   e.g. *Bus*, coat, tree, *car*, *train*.
5. *Inferences.* A problem is given which requires reasoning for its solution.
   e.g. Sally is taller than Jill.
   Jill is taller than Stan.
   Who is taller, Sally or Stan?

Other types of items, for example, codes, ordering, number or letter series, may also be included in verbal tests (see Lovell 1967). When the subject has to select the correct answer from a number of possible answers, the item is known as a multiple-choice item. When the subject has to supply the answer, it is known as a creative-response or open-ended item. Verbal tests may consist exclusively of one or the other type of item or include both types.

A test which is strictly verbal will be influenced by the subject's level of reading attainment and his familiarity with language; that is to say, performance on verbal tests will be affected if the subject has not had normal opportunities to acquire language skills. There is evidence that the culturally deprived child, the child of itinerant parents, the partially hearing child and the non-English-speaking immigrant child are generally unlikely to perform well on verbal tests.

Non-verbal tests consist of problems which are presented in the form of abstract diagrams or pictures and which rely very little on familiarity with language or with level of reading attainment. The thinking skills tested are similar to those tested by means of verbal tests and include items involving analogies, similarities, coding and series. However, few non-verbal tests are entirely independent of language, since the directions are invariably verbal, and the subject is also likely to use language when thinking about the problems he is required to solve. Thus those children whose language experience is limited are still likely to be handicapped on some non-verbal tests (see Vernon 1968). Non-verbal tests have not proved to correlate as highly as verbal tests with general scholastic performance or to predict it as accurately. They have, however, been found to be useful predictors for vocational guidance purposes.

Group tests of mental ability are very widely used in research, but from the foregoing discussion it can be seen that they possess certain limitations. It follows that care must be shown in the choice of a group test which is suited to the aims of the research. If two groups of subjects are to be compared for level of mental ability, it is better to use an individual test if possible in order to make the comparison.

Tests which have been devised for use with groups can often be administered to individual subjects, but, as already stated, some tests of mental ability have been especially constructed for use with individuals. They are not normally available to teachers, chiefly because of the complexity of the test and the difficulty of the interpretation of the results. Individual tests are extremely valuable for use with children who for a number of reasons may not be capable of performing optimally in response to a group test. Children who are below the age of seven years or who are emotionally disturbed, or physically handicapped, or who experience difficulty in reading and writing, are likely to be assessed more accurately by means of an individual test of mental ability. Where any decision has to be taken in relation to a child's educational placement, an individual test is indicated, but for screening purposes or for sequential decisions, a group test may suffice.

An individual test widely used for assessment in this country is the third revision of the Stanford-Binet Scale (Terman and Merrill 1959). This is the latest in a series of versions of the original Binet-Simon Intelligence Scale which was first published in France in 1905. For a full description of the different versions reference should be made to the manuals which accompany each test. For briefer descriptions and evaluations of the more recent versions reference should be made to Buros (1965) and Cronbach (1960).

It is important to realize that even the most recent version of the Stanford-Binet is a test which has been adapted for use and standardized in the United States of America and that its use for guidance and research purposes in Great Britain poses certain difficulties. The other widely used individual tests of mental ability are the Wechsler Adult Intelligence Scale (WAIS) and the Wechsler Intelligence Scale for Children (WISC), both of which were constructed by Wechsler. The most recent versions of the tests were published in 1952 and 1949 respectively. The tests are similar in design, the items in each being divided into a verbal and a performance sub-scale. The verbal half of the test is composed of a number of sub-tests which are verbal in character, whilst the performance part is composed of an equal number of practical sub-tests. Separate quotients can be obtained for each sub-scale, as well as a quotient for performance on the test as a whole.

Individual tests should not be used for research purposes by those who are untrained and inexperienced in their use; otherwise errors are likely to occur. In evaluating the findings of any research study in which individual tests have been used, attention must be paid to possible sources of error which may exist in the tests, as well as the characteristics of the sample to whom the tests were given and the experience of those who administered them.

APTITUDE TESTS

An aptitude may be thought of as the ability to acquire special types of skill or knowledge, and those tests which have been designed to determine special abilities are called aptitude tests. Tests have been devised to assess specific mental abilities such as mechanical and manipulative skills, artistic and musical potential, and aptitude for specific vocational fields such as language, medicine and science.

They measure present performance in areas in which no specific training has been given in an attempt to predict the degree of achievement which may be expected if training is given. The view has been expressed that they are assessing innate potential—that tests of musical aptitude, for example, measure the basic innate capacities involved in musical activities. In a recent article, however, Vernon (1968) argues persuasively against the idea that innate potentiality can be measured independently of experience and past learning. In relation to musical aptitude tests in particular, he suggests that these are sampling 'certain low-level skills as developed up to that time, which following on further experience and training, may be integrated into higher-level musical skills'.

The value of aptitude tests has been widely questioned, the view being taken that, whilst they do measure achievement in a specialized area, they may not be any more effective for predictive purposes in that area than tests of general mental ability and attainment. Only a few tests have been devised to assess aptitudes in any given area and some of these are badly designed and technically unsophisticated. It is apparent that much more research is needed in order to assess more accurately the contribution that aptitude tests can make to the gathering of research data.

TESTS OF ATTAINMENT

Tests of attainment or achievement have been constructed to measure present performance in relation to a skill or knowledge which has been acquired as a result of training or tuition. Tests are available to measure performance in many areas, in particular the basic educational subjects of mathematics and English. They are widely used for educational assessment, selection and guidance. By measuring present attainment they are among the best predictors of future attainment.

Many attainment tests have been devised but not all of them are good ones. The large majority of those which have been published are described and evaluated in the *Mental Measurement Yearbooks* (e.g. Buros 1965). Many group tests of attainment have been published by the National Foundation for Educational Research and many experienced teachers will be familiar with some of them. The difficulties associated with group tests of mental ability must be kept in mind, for these apply with equal force to group tests of attainment. It is especially important to realize that some group tests, even those which measure attainment in mathematics, demand a minimum level of reading ability and in this sense measure attainment in reading as well as the subject with which the test is chiefly concerned.

Many group tests of attainment can be given to individual subjects, but some tests have been specifically devised for use with individual subjects. Certain skills, for example, oral reading skills, can only be measured by means of tests which are administered individually.

Attainment tests are widely used for research purposes, and in evaluating the findings of studies in which they have been used, attention must be paid to the appropriateness of their use with the sample studies, and the reliability and validity of the tests. Many tests have been designed for use only with a restricted age range and have not been standardized on children of other age groups. Others have been devised to measure only one aspect of attainment and have no general applicability.

Since attainment tests attempt to measure the effect of tuition, it is important to realize that if the content of a subject is changed or the sequence of topics in the subject is altered, the test items, which were originally selected on the basis of their coverage of the content of a subject, may not continue to carry out this function. At the present time, for example, the content of mathematics and the sequence in which the topics are being taught is undergoing considerable change, and it is quite possible that tests which are at least five years old may not be measuring those topics in mathematics which are now being taught in the schools. In view of these considerations the findings of research studies which have used attainment tests must be carefully examined in order to assess the appropriateness of tests and their relevance to current thinking and ideas.

CHAPTER 6

Instruments of research 2: self-report techniques

Self-report techniques have been devised to collect information on an individual's feelings, interests and personality traits, also on his relationships with his peer groups, by requiring him to reply to a series of questions about these aspects of his behaviour. Some of these techniques are concerned with ascertaining the nature and the dimensions of his attitudes and beliefs that are held concerning issues, institutions, and activities in society. Others list the interests which he has in relation to particular activities or occupations, or seek information on his personality characteristics, while yet others assess the nature of the social relationships which are present amongst members of a group. Techniques included in this category and which will be discussed in this chapter include questionnaires, inventories, projective techniques, scales and sociometric techniques.

Questionnaires

Questionnaires are widely used in education to obtain information about current conditions and practices and to make inquiries concerning attitudes and opinions. In *A Dictionary of Psychology*, Drever (1956) defines a questionnaire as 'a series of questions dealing with some psychological, social, educational, etc., topic or topics, sent or given to a group of individuals, with the object of obtaining data with regard to some problems; sometimes employed for diagnostic purposes, or for assessing *personality traits*'. In fact, any formally organized list of questions which are presented in a uniform manner to a number of persons is a questionnaire, and in certain circumstances this is the most effective method of eliciting information.

A questionnaire has the advantage of applying certain restrictions upon a situation:

1. It asks specific questions which call for specific answers.
2. These answers can be classified.
3. The information contained in the responses can sometimes be quantified.

Thus the questionnaire has the advantage of providing information quickly, and in a precise form.

Not all human beings, however, respond to this situation. Some may be unable to express themselves in words, others may be unwilling, or may not be qualified to provide the information which is sought. Certain questions may be ignored and answers to others may be falsified. This is especially true if the self-interests of the respondents appear to be attacked, or if they feel the need to protect themselves, to please the research worker, or to conform to what they consider are socially acceptable forms of behaviour. Such behaviour is most likely to be found in respect of those questionnaires which seek information which is subjective in character—the type which is concerned with personal opinions, judgements, attitudes and feelings. Those who design questionnaires which seek such information must continually guard against this form of behaviour.

TYPES OF QUESTIONNAIRES

One way of classifying questionnaires is in terms of the information which is being sought, so one type of questionnaire is that which seeks information which is known only to the respondent; for example, information about his attitudes and beliefs. It is very difficult indeed to check such information by reference to any other source. A second type is more objective, seeking to obtain factual information. Some of these might seek information on past events concerning which most respondents will have kept no written records; for example, a mother may be asked to recall the major steps in her child's development. Others might seek information on present conditions which is readily available to the respondents; for example, a head-teacher may be asked to supply information on the methods used in his school to teach reading. The last type of questionnaire may seek information on past or present events for which written records have been made and which could be used to check the information given by the respondent; for example, information supplied by a head-teacher on pupils' attendance could be checked by reference to written records of attendance.

Another way in which questionnaires may be classified is in terms of the nature of the questions which are used. Questions may be asked in a *closed* or an *open* form, and a researcher may use one type exclusively or both in combination. Questionnaires which consist of a set of questions to which the respondent can reply in a limited number of ways is a *closed* type of questionnaire. The respondent is invariably permitted to reply only with 'yes' or 'no', or 'no opinion', or is requested to select an answer from a short list of possible responses. He may do this by placing a tick in a space provided on the answer sheet or he may be requested to tick or underline a response. Sometimes he is asked to insert brief answers of his own. The following example illustrates the closed type of question:

Are you in favour of comprehensive education?
Underline one of the following answers.
Yes. No. No opinion.

The closed form of questionnaire is easy to administer and easy for the respondent to complete. It also has the advantage of keeping the respondent on the subject with the result that the responses can be tabulated and analysed with a minimum of difficulty. However, the fixed alternative responses may have the effect of forcing the subject to reply in a way in which he would not have thought of doing had he been left to give his own words. For this reason it is useful to provide a certain degree of freedom by permitting the respondent to qualify his answer if he is dissatisfied with the alternatives he is given. It is quite possible that in this way a reply will be obtained which the investigator did not anticipate when drawing up the list of possible answers.

The *open* form of questionnaire contains questions to which the respondent can reply as he likes and where he is not limited to a single alternative. Open questions are not followed by any kind of choice and the answers have to be supplied and written by the respondent. The major advantage of this type of question is the freedom that is given to the subject to reveal his attitudes or motives, and to qualify or clarify his answers. The open question evokes a richer and fuller response and probably probes more deeply than the closed question.

There are certain disadvantages associated with the open question. Open questions are often easier to phrase than closed questions, but they may be more difficult to answer. Respondents may find it difficult to reply without the help of clues to guide their thinking, especially if they are not particularly intelligent, or if the questionnaire is designed to elicit information about a subject with which they are unfamiliar, or seeks their opinions on an issue on which they have no views. Conversely, some subjects will find little difficulty in providing a wealth of information, but the tabulation and interpretation of this may be both difficult and time consuming.

Sometimes questionnaires include both open and closed questions. Often there may be good reasons for asking the same question in both open and closed forms. In his response to the open question the subject will express his own thoughts on the topic in his own words, and this response can be contrasted with his responses to the closed question where his reply will be restricted by the list of fixed alternative answers. In practice a good questionnaire should include both forms of questions, especially if a deep and thorough knowledge of the facts is required. The results of the one type can be checked with the other and will illuminate the subject under inquiry in different ways.

THE SCOPE OF A QUESTIONNAIRE

The actual scope of a questionnaire is wider than most people realize, for all form filling is really answering some form of questionnaire. They can range from the ballot paper, which usually consists of only one or two specific questions each of which is followed by a number of alternative replies, to a list of questions in answer to which the respondent may write essays. The former type is best used for the superficial study of large groups and is very easy to score, whilst the latter type is best used where a few individuals have to be intensively investigated, but it presents difficulties in scoring and interpretation.

PREPARATION OF THE QUESTIONNAIRE

In the investigation of a research problem, the investigator must give some consideration to the collection of the data. There are a number of ways in which this can be done and he must select the one which is most appropriate for his needs. If the questionnaire is selected, the precise nature and the amount of the information which is sought must be decided upon, for it is advisable to keep the questionnaire as brief as possible. There is no purpose in collecting more information than is actually needed and a long questionnaire may well go unanswered. This is especially true if the purpose of the questions appears vague to the respondent and if the wording of the questions is ambiguous. The completion of a questionnaire is a courtesy which is asked of people, and it should be formulated and administered in such a way that the results are collected with the minimum expenditure of the respondent's time, and yield a maximum amount of data for the time expended.

Efforts must be made to gain the co-operation of the respondents, for upon this depends the success of the inquiry. The topic with which the inquiry is concerned should be seen by the respondent as important enough for him to spend his time completing it. The completion of a questionnaire demands the respondent's time no matter how brief it may be, and it is important that he is not asked nor forced to spend time on something that he regards as trivial. The respondents will be more favourably disposed towards the inquiry if its purpose and the nature of the topic are stated on the questionnaire or on the letter which accompanies it. In many inquiries in which questionnaires are used there is often no feedback to the respondents, yet many are often interested in the topic being investigated and in the findings of a piece of research in which they have been involved. Whilst it is clearly not possible to report findings to all respondents as a matter of course, consideration must be given to dispensing information to those who wish to receive it; otherwise the incentive to co-operate in future research may not be forthcoming.

A good deal of research in education involves the use of school children as subjects and it is important to obtain the permission of the appropriate authorities, including the head-teachers of the schools concerned. Furthermore, it may be advisable to obtain the permission of the parents. This is often forgotten, but no research worker has the right to use a child for research purposes without their permission. Education officials are concerned to protect school children from exploitation, since children primarily attend school for reasons other than to act as subjects for research. For this and other reasons access is often restricted to those whose research is being sponsored by educational institutions or government agencies.

There is always the possibility that questionnaires which are designed to elicit information from respondents which may damage their self-interests may not be truthfully answered. If the information sought is of this type, care must be taken to assure the subjects that the information supplied will be held in strict confidence. It may be necessary to allow for anonymous responses, since this method is most likely to gain the confidence of the respondent. The view is sometimes put forward that no subjects should be asked to supply information which may not be in their self-interest, nor should they be asked questions about their relatives and friends. Whatever view is held in this matter, it is important to bear in mind that in answering questions relating to these topics respondents are always likely to provide untruthful replies.

The instructions used in questionnaires must be clear and complete, and couched in terms that all the respondents can understand. Particular care must be taken to ensure that information is given as to where the responses should be made and in what form, and subjects should not have to work this out for themselves. Ambiguity in the instructions will lead to different interpretations being placed upon them by different subjects, and this will lead to different results.

DESIGNING THE QUESTIONNAIRE

Designing a questionnaire is a complex and involved operation. The nature, form and order of the questions is of great importance if meaningful results are to be obtained. Asking questions that will elicit the precise data required is no easy task, and unless great care is taken to foresee sources of ambiguity in phrasing, difficulties will occur in the interpretation of the results. It is the experience of research workers that respondents often draw many different meanings from questions which appeared to be unambiguous. It is, of course, very difficult to phrase questions in such a way that no one can misinterpret them, but every effort must be made to frame them in as precise a way as possible.

A pilot study can be most useful in devising the actual wording of questions, for quite often ambiguities in the questions will be revealed by the nature of the replies which are obtained. One advantage of presenting questions in an interview situation is that it allows misunderstandings to be cleared up, but the written question which calls for a written reply must stand by itself; much of the criticism of the questionnaire as a method of collecting information has occurred as a result of the inferior way in which questions have been formulated.

Whilst entirely unambiguous questions are difficult to phrase, there are certain principles which an investigator might follow to word them as precisely as possible. Sometimes terms or words are likely to be misinterpreted, and these must be anticipated and clearly defined. One such group of words are those which are used in relation to time. Words such as 'often', 'occasionally' and 'seldom' have no agreed meaning, and they will be interpreted differently by different persons. One subject's 'often' may be the equivalent of another's 'occasionally', and another's 'seldom' the equivalent of another's 'often'. In order to avoid these different interpretations a stated frequency of occurrence—say, times per day or week—is preferable.

The use of complex questions should also be avoided, since these can lead to confusion and difficulty in interpretation. The question 'Have you taught English and mathematics in the last two terms?' is complex, and a fixed alternative answer of yes or no would not suffice. In reality two separate questions are being asked, 'Have you taught English in the last two terms?' and 'Have you taught mathematics in the last two terms?,' and in order to avoid confusion they should be presented to the subjects as two separate questions.

In constructing closed questions care must be taken to ensure that the permitted alternatives actually exhaust the number of possible answers. The following is an example of a poor question:

Which method do you use to teach reading?
Underline one of the following:
1. Phonic Word
2. Initial Teaching Alphabet
3. Colour Story Reading

The three alternatives provided do not exhaust the number of possible answers, since there are other methods of teaching reading which might be used by the respondent. Moreover, the Initial Teaching Alphabet (apart from Colour Story Reading) provides a medium for teaching but not a method.

THE ORDER OF QUESTIONS IN THE QUESTIONNAIRE

A questionnaire is not a series of questions presented in any order. It should be a series of questions in which their order-number and grouping must be carefully considered.

The order in which questions are posed is important. They should not offend the subject, thus making him adopt a defensive attitude towards the inquiry, nor should they contaminate one another. The difficulties posed by inquiries which seek information of a delicate nature have already been referred to. Certain questions which may disturb the respondent can increase the number of non-responses and can contaminate the questions which follow. There are some techniques for overcoming or trying to overcome such an eventuality.

1. Questions on certain matters are always likely to be answered untruthfully and this must be recognized by the research worker, and techniques for checking the responses, such as lie scales, must be built into the questionnaire.
2. Questions of a nature which will disturb or upset the

subject can be placed at, or near, the end of the series of questions so that if the subject is upset and is unable to co-operate his earlier responses will not be contaminated.

3. Questions dealing with topics which may upset the respondents can be worded in a way which will cause the least embarrassment, but which will still reveal the information which is sought. For example, respondents may not wish to reveal too much about their income by replying to a questionnaire. A direct question which asks for the amount earned to be stated may not produce an honest answer, but much the same sort of knowledge can be acquired in an oblique way by asking about material possessions which will allow inferences to be drawn about the subject's income.

THE NUMBER OF QUESTIONS IN THE QUESTIONNAIRE

A questionnaire should not be any longer than is necessary. Consideration must therefore be given to the total number of questions to be included and also to the number of questions to be asked about the same topic.

The total number of questions must not be so many as to tire or bore the respondent. This is especially important if the subjects are children. If too many questions are asked and the subjects become tired, the questions at the end of the series may not be well answered. It is difficult to state the most suitable number of questions—to a certain extent this depends upon the nature of the topic being investigated and the character of the subjects. A questionnaire given to subjects who have all received higher education can possibly be longer than that put to subjects who left school at the end of secondary education, if one assumes that the former group are more familiar, and have been more recently in contact, with a task which calls for the interpretation of verbal material. A total of thirty questions is an optimum number—a larger number could be presented as two separate questionnaires. If the questions can easily be interpreted and only require one-word answers the total could exceed thirty. However, if a considerable degree of interpretation is involved, fewer than thirty questions is desirable.

ADMINISTRATION OF A QUESTIONNAIRE

To some extent the way in which a questionnaire is administered depends upon the nature of replies which are sought. In the planning stage some thought must be given to the way in which the questionnaire will be administered and to the abilities of people to whom it will be given. The questionnaire can call for written or oral replies. Some questionnaires are designed with the intention that they should be answered in writing, others are designed in a way which requires an oral response.

Questionnaires which require written replies are presented in one of two ways: either by post or in a group situation such as a class of children.

POSTAL QUESTIONNAIRES

There are obvious advantages in this kind of administration, but there are also certain limitations. Mailed questionnaires can be despatched to a large sample scattered over a wide geographical area quickly and relatively cheaply. In certain research situations where a representative sample is sought it is often necessary to contact a widely scattered group, and the postal questionnaire offers distinct advantages. A second point to be made in favour of postal questionnaires is that some respondents prefer the lack of physical contact with an interviewer or prefer to complete the questionnaire at a time which is convenient for them.

A serious disadvantage attached to questionnaires sent by post is the proportion of non-replies which occur. Usually only a small percentage of replies are forthcoming even from groups which in other respects are known to be conscientious. Returns ranging from 10 to 40 per cent of the sample are not uncommon, whilst returns of 60 per cent or over must be considered to be very high. Needless to say, the smaller the percentage of responses, the smaller is the degree of confidence which can be placed in the adequacy of the data which has been collected. Furthermore, there is also some likelihood that those who replied are different in some way from those who did not. It is possible that they may be less well educated or less interested in the topic than those who responded, and this may introduce a bias that will render the data useless. The difficulty is that this form of administration demands a personal effort on the part of the respondents, and it must be expected that some will be unwilling to make that effort and that others will be unable to reply because they have not achieved the level of literacy required to read and answer the questionnaire.

A further limitation is that there can be a time lapse between the time the questionnaire is received and read, and the time it is completed. The longer the time interval the greater is the chance that the respondent will be influenced by events which occur during the interval. He may attempt to acquire knowledge by consulting books, or he may change his original views as a result of discussing the questions with his friends. In either case his replies are likely to be different from those he would have made had he completed the questionnaire as soon as he received it.

There are steps which can be taken to overcome to some extent the disadvantages attached to postal questionnaires. The major disadvantage, the low response rate, could be anticipated in the research design. A first step would be to consider the character of the respondents, and to gather information about them including whether they are likely to respond to a questionnaire sent by post. Questionnaires could then be sent to a larger number of subjects than is required for the purposes of the study in order to counteract the inevitable proportion of non-responses.

Once the questionnaire has been sent out, a follow-up could be staged which could involve the use of postcards reminding those who have not responded that they have not done so.

GROUP QUESTIONNAIRES

Questionnaires which call for written replies may also be administered to groups in a face-to-face situation. The role to be played by the person in charge ought to be defined in the research design, but no matter how passive his role he is likely to influence the respondents by his appearance and manner. This form of administration also has certain advantages. It usually leads to a low non-response rate, and distortions introduced by time lapses are likely to be minimized. It is a valuable way of administering questionnaires in educational research.

Questionnaires which call for written replies are best used for the collection of factual information rather than opinions, from samples whose characteristics are known.

ORAL REPLIES

Questionnaires which call for oral replies are usually presented to one subject at a time in an interview. The use of the interview method of collecting data will be discussed later in chapter 7.

VALUE OF THE RESULTS OF A QUESTIONNAIRE

The value of the results—the extent to which they reflect reality—depends upon many factors, including the quality of the questions. Several sources of error in the use of questionnaires have already been discussed. These include errors which are due to faulty design, inadequate sampling, high non-response rates and the presence and influence of interviewers. Errors can also occur if the subjects do not reply truthfully, and if inappropriate statistical techniques are used in the analysis of the results.

A further source of error now to be considered relates to the reliability and validity of the questionnaire which is used to collect the data. Reliability refers to consistency, to obtaining the same results on a second occasion. Thus a questionnaire may be said to be reliable if, when it is applied to the same subjects at different times by the same investigator, it gives similar results. Its reliability can be measured by calculating the correlation between the two sets of results and obtaining the coefficient of reliability. If oral replies are obtained to a questionnaire presented in an interview by an interviewer who will interpret the replies, the reliability of the interviewer must also be considered. In these circumstances a questionnaire would be reliable if similar results were obtained after it had been presented to the same subjects at different times by different investigators. If the time interval between the two administrations is short, subjects may remember items and their responses may be influenced. On the other hand, if the time interval is long, a change in behaviour may have occurred. In either of these circumstances there may be a differenee in the two sets of results obtained. There are other factors which must also be considered in relation to the reliability of a questionnaire, but these are too technical for inclusion in this book and reference should be made to Oppenheim (1966).

To be reliable a questionnaire has only to measure accurately and consistently, but to be valid it must measure whatever it is supposed to measure. The method of determining the validity of questionnaires, as with other research instruments, is by comparing the results obtained with some external criteria. One such criterion might be the results obtained from the direct observation of the behaviour of the respondents. For example, if a questionnaire seeks information on church attendance, the results could be checked by observations of what subjects actually did on Sundays. Documentary evidence can also be used in a similar manner to check the results of a questionnaire, or reports of the actual behaviour can be obtained from another person. The opinions of experts in the field being investigated must also be sought on whether a questionnaire measures what it claims to measure. They should be aware of the area which the questionnaire seeks to cover, and be in a position to offer advice on the value of the results obtained.

It is, of course, possible to compare the questionnaire results obtained with previous research findings. This applies chiefly to areas of research which have been relatively well explored. If there are serious differences when the findings are compared the validity of the questionnaire may be in doubt, or the samples studied may differ greatly in composition.

CONCLUSION

Questionnaires appear to be relatively easy to construct, but there are hazards which must be taken into account. There are many sources of error and the questionnaire is not a perfect instrument. However, it has the advantage of providing information especially that of a subjective nature, which is difficult to obtain in any other way. Where distortions occur, the cause of the distortions may be important and could provide the basis of further research.

Inventories

An inventory is constructed in the form of a questionnaire; in fact, the terms 'inventory' and 'questionnaire' appear to be used interchangeably. It consists of a series of questions or statements to which the individual must respond by answering 'yes' or 'no', 'agree' or 'disagree', or in some similar way indicate his opinions or feelings. The list of items relates to the factor being appraised, which may be, say, scholastic or vocational interests, or personality traits. The subject is required to indicate preferences or to mark those items that describe his typical behaviour. The research worker evaluates the responses to obtain descriptions of certain fundamental predispositions of the subject.

Inventories have been constructed to provide information on the strength and direction of a subject's interests, attitudes and values, and these represent an important aspect of the personality. Although individual inventories have been designed to provide information specifically on either interests, or attitudes, or personality traits, there is the possibility that they overlap to some extent.

The inventory has been widely used for the investigation of interests, but increasing use is being made of this approach in the assessment of personality. An interest may be defined as an individual's tendency to be attracted towards a particular object or activity. Inventories which are used to investigate interests usually require the subject to respond to questions which seek information on his preferences or his dislikes. Whilst many inventories have been devised, Cronbach (1960) refers to three main approaches to inventory construction: empirical keying, homogeneous keying, and logical keying, and suggests that there is evidence that the three types measure approximately the same interests.

Interest inventories were originally constructed for vocational guidance and they are chiefly used today for the same purpose, although some have been devised for educational guidance. These are used in an attempt to differentiate between academic and practical or technical interests. The two best-known British ones are the *General Information Test* and the *Devon Interest Test*. The former test was developed by Lambert and Peel (Peel 1948) and measures interest in academic and practical pursuits by assessing the amount of knowledge displayed by the respondent about the topic of interest. The *Devon Interest Test*, devised by Wiseman and Fitzpatrick (1955), assesses the relative strengths of interest shown in academic and practical activities by investigating the subjects' 'likes' and 'dislikes'. Others have been specifically devised for educational guidance purposes, but the value of such inventories has yet to be determined (Yates and Barr 1960).

As with other self-report techniques, valid results will not be obtained if the individual does not provide truthful replies. There is also an indication that the predictive validity of the results will not be high if the subjects tested are below seventeen years of age, since studies by Strong (1943) suggest that interests are not stable until this age is attained.

Increasing use is being made of the inventory to assess personality traits, although as yet not many have been constructed. A typical personality inventory consists of a series of questions, e.g. 'Do you get upset easily?' or 'Do you find it difficult to make friends?' The subject responds by selecting one of the alternative answers which are provided. The score may be in terms of a single adjustment score, or in terms of a separate score for particular adjustment areas, e.g. social or emotional, or for specific personality traits, e.g. sociability, self-confidence.

Inventories which have been constructed for use with adults and which have been used for clinical experimental studies and applied work, include the *Eysenck Personality Inventory* (Eysenck and Eysenck 1963), which is designed to measure neuroticism and extraversion-introversion, and the *Sixteen Personality Factor Inventory* (Cattell 1957). Those designed for use with children include the *Junior Eysenck Personality Inventory* (Eysenck 1965), which has been designed to measure extraversion-introversion and neuroticism-stability and the *High School Personality Questionnaire* devised by Cattell and Beloff (1962), which, it is claimed, assesses fourteen independent factors including emotional maturity, super-ego strength and anxiety level.

In evaluating the findings of research studies which have made use of personality inventories several factors relating to the validity of the results must be kept in mind. Many of the most recently constructed inventories are extremely reliable, but they are usually constructed on the basis of a particular theory of the organization of personality and it must be remembered that there are a number of theories of personality organization, none of which appears to include all the known facts and is generally acceptable. The value of the results depends also upon the individual's willingness to co-operate and to produce truthful answers, and upon his awareness of his motives, some of which may be unconscious. In an attempt to overcome the faking of replies some inventories include a lie scale or a control key, but there is some doubt as to whether faking or untruthfulness can be entirely overcome by this means. Finally, as in all techniques which pose questions, the interpretation of the questions by the subjects will vary according to the characteristics of the subjects and the wording of the questions (for a fuller discussion see the section on questionnaires).

Projective techniques

Projective techniques are used to investigate areas of personality that cannot be reached easily by other means, or areas in which direct questions are unlikely to be answered truthfully. Instead of being required to supply specific information as in a personality inventory, typically the individual is presented with ambiguous stimuli such as pictures, inkblots, words and unfinished sentences, and is asked to describe or to interpret what he sees, or to complete the sentences. The individual is usually free to follow his own phantasies and inclinations; however, a minority of techniques pose a series of questions relating to the stimuli in order to elicit information.

The use of the projective technique is based on the assumption that the individual will unconsciously interpret situations and events by reading into them his own feelings and experiences. It is supposed that as a consequence of the ambiguity of the stimuli and the freedom from restraint, the individual's total personality pattern will be revealed; to this end his responses are analysed to determine what structure he has projected on to the ambiguous stimuli.

The analysis of the responses usually entails only subjective interpretation by the investigator, but in a minority of techniques some form of scoring procedure is also used. The interpretation of the responses often demands a high degree of skill and a prolonged period of training. Projective techniques are difficult to validate and few have been standardized. The *Rorschach Inkblot Test* and the *Thematic Apperception Test* are the two most extensively used with adults, and the *Family Attitudes Test* (Jackson 1957) and the *Controlled Projection Test* (Raven 1951) are the two most extensively used with children.

Attitude scales

Much of the data of the behavioural sciences cannot easily be expressed in standardized units which convey the same meaning to everyone. But since precise measurement is the key to scientific progress, a number of scaling techniques have been developed which permit numerical values or ratings to be assigned to some kind of subjective judgement or estimate of the size of variables.

Scales have been devised for use in two main ways: (1) for rating the behaviour of a person or aspects of a thing, for example, the quality of the fixtures and furnishings of a home or school; (2) for the evaluation of attitudes by means of a questionnaire prepared in the form of a scale, and presented in an interview (individual or group) or sent through the post. Attitudes can be evaluated in either, or both of these ways, that is to say by means of observation or by the use of self-report attitude scales which are designed to measure the extent to which an individual has favourable or unfavourable feelings towards some person, object, issue or institution.

The scale technique has been widely used for the evaluation of attitudes and many different types of scale have been developed, including the equal-appearing intervals scale, the method of graded dichotomies, the method of summated ratings, scalogram analysis, scale discrimination technique, etc., all of which are described by Shaw and Wright (1967). We shall be mainly concerned with the two most widely used scales, the equal-appearing intervals scale and the method of summated ratings.

The *equal-appearing intervals scale* was originally devised by Thurstone and Chave (1929) and has been modified subsequently in the light of experience. The procedure to be described is similar but not identical to that devised by Thurstone and Chave, and it includes the following steps:

1. A large number of statements which express varying degrees of intensity of feeling or opinion towards an issue, object or institution are collected.
2. The statements are then given to thirty or more judges, who preferably should be similar to those subjects to whom the finished scale will be applied. Each judge is informed of the purpose of the scale and is asked to sort the statements into categories (usually seven to eleven) according to whether they appear to him to represent a favourable, neutral, or unfavourable attitude to the factor being evaluated.
3. As a result of the sorting procedure the distribution of sortings of each statement by all the judges is examined, and its position obtained. If there is marked disagreement between the judges in the placement of a statement, it is discarded as being irrelevent or ambiguous. Each statement which is retained is given a scale value which is based on the median position assigned it by the judges.
4. The final form of the scale is then constructed by selecting twenty to thirty of the statements which are most relevant, least ambiguous, and which cover or represent the different intensities of the attitude. They are then arranged in random order.

5. The scale is then administered and subjects are asked to indicate the statements with which they are in agreement and the median of the scale values of the statements is their score for the attitude. For a fuller description of this method reference should be made to Oppenheim (1966) or Evans (1965).

The method of *summated ratings* which can be used without judges was introduced by Likert (1932). This method appears to yield similar results to that devised by Thurstone and Chave and, since it is much simpler, it tends to be used more frequently. A large number of statements, which indicate a position for or against a particular issue are collected and presented in the form of a preliminary scale to a group of subjects. The subjects are required to respond to each statement on a five-point scale: strongly agree, agree, undecided, disagree, and strongly disagree. For scoring purposes the five positions are arbitrarily given weights of 5 to 1, the highest value always being given to the responses that demonstrate the greatest degree of favourableness to the topic. The total score for each subject is the sum of the values assigned to each item that he marked. The scores for each item are then correlated with the total score and only those that correlate highly are selected for the final scale.

It has been claimed that Likert's method of attitude assessment is the more reliable (Edwards 1957), but the view is taken here that it is impossible to say which of the two methods of attitude assessment is best used for research. Both have been devised for slightly different purposes and have important desirable features as well as certain limitations. It is the task of the research worker to acquaint himself with the characteristics of each scale and then attempt to evaluate the contribution that each might make to the solution of his own particular research problem.

Attempts have been made to validate attitude scales by comparing them with older scales and also by correlating the results with actual behaviour. The former approach has been widely used and a high degree of correlation has been found between certain scales. This does not mean, however, that the validity of the older scales has been established. The latter approach has also been made use of and it has been shown that the predictive value of attitude scales in relation to behaviour is not high. This is probably because the causes of behaviour are complex and attitudes may play only a small part in determining it, but it is also almost certainly the case that attitude scales are only measuring the expressed opinions of individuals and not the attitudes which they actually hold.

Sociometric techniques

Sociometry is a technique used for describing the social relationships which exist among members of a group. Essentially the technique involves asking each member of a group to indicate in order of preference which other members he would prefer to associate with in a particular activity and which of them he rejects. It therefore takes the form of a simple questionnaire and makes use of an ordinal scale in that the preferences are placed in rank order.

The choices made may be plotted on a sociogram. Each member of the group is represented by a symbol, say, a circle for a girl, a triangle for a boy, and the relationships which exist are represented by the use of connecting lines, which are solid for acceptance and broken for rejection. This technique thus represents graphically the degree of cohesiveness of the group, its sub-groupings or cliques, and those members who are popular or who are rejected by their fellow group members. For a fuller description of this technique reference should be made to Moreno (1953) or Northway and Weld (1957).

It must be realized that the pattern of relations obtained in this way are relative to the group in which they were obtained. If the same group are subjected to a new situation or to new experiences, or if the composition of the group is changed, a different pattern of relationships may emerge.

Whilst the notion of reliability and validity may not apply directly to sociometric techniques (cf. Lindzey and Borgatta 1959), most of the reported studies dealing with the relation of the results obtained by the use of sociometry to actual behaviour show moderately high correlations. As with the measurement of attitudes, however, it is probable that behaviour in social situations depends upon many factors and that the sociometric technique assesses only one of these factors—the expressed preferences and rejections of members of a group.

CHAPTER 7

Instruments of research 3: observational techniques

In certain types of research problem information can best be obtained by means of the observation of behaviour. This is done either *directly*, as when the investigator plays a passive role and observes without intervening in any way, or in an *interview*, where the investigator plays a more active role, perhaps by asking a series of questions or administering a test, and where he observes the behaviour of the interviewee as well as recording his responses.

Direct observational methods

The direct observation of behaviour is a particularly useful form of data collection, especially when other research techniques are unavailable or inappropriate. It has a valuable part to play in collecting information on behaviour in naturally occurring situations such as the play of children, or on the pattern or degree of social interaction amongst groups of human beings. Indeed, many investigators believe that the important patterns of human behaviour can only be obtained by observing behaviour when it occurs naturally under conditions in which the subject reacts to those factors which are significant for him. The behaviour of teachers in the classroom can only be effectively analysed by observing how they behave in an actual classroom.

The observation of behaviour in this way does not imply a

lack of procedure. When used for research purposes it should be carried out by an experienced person for a specific purpose and the data must be collected in a systematic manner. As with other research methods, its accuracy, validity and reliability must be checked. Furthermore, the research worker must be able to distinguish between the significant aspects of behaviour and those which are of little importance. He must also be capable of objectivity, and of carefully measuring and recording the data. There are many devices which serve to focus his attention on specific phenomena. There are others which aid him in the accurate and objective collection of data, and there are some which enable him to collect his observations systematically.

THE TIME SAMPLING METHOD

The direct observation of behaviour poses certain problems, one of these being the question of the period of time over which behaviour is to be studied. Often the purpose of direct observation is to determine the nature of typical behaviour, but behaviour can vary over long periods of time. However, since it is not usually possible, because of the expense, to observe behaviour continuously for long periods, a technique known as time sampling has been widely used in research studies. For examples of its use with primary school pupils see Gardner (1950). By this technique behaviour can be studied for a number of short periods of time which are systematically spaced over the total period of study. A child's behaviour, for example, or certain aspects of it may be studied for the whole of a school day by means of a series of observations each of five minutes' duration, made at intervals of a quarter of an hour. It is feasible to study children over long periods of time by this means, and it is probably the case that a series of short, well-distributed observations provides a more typical picture of behaviour than a few longer periods of observation.

THE INCIDENT SAMPLING METHOD

Another observational method of gathering data is incident sampling. This technique, which is similar in design to anecdotal records, concerns the observation of the behaviour of an individual in selected incidents or situations in which he becomes involved. It entails the observation of certain instances of selected behaviour rather than behaviour in selected situations. For example, an investigator may observe and report on those occasions in which an individual exhibits certain forms of behaviour, e.g. when he laughs or cries. In addition to providing a factual account of the behaviour of the individual in the incident, a description is given of the kind of situation in which the behaviour occurred and of the nature of any precipitating stimulus which led to the behaviour. The response of the individual to the stimulus is described and its intensity and duration are recorded. After a series of such observations an investigator may have sufficient data to draw inferences about the typical pattern of behaviour of the individual.

The observations made in both time and incident sampling will be of little value unless the facts are reported as objectively as possible and systematically recorded. In order to do this, use can be made of mechanical instruments such as cameras and tape recorders to assist in the reporting of behaviour, and the information can be stored on record cards. It is important that the factual description of behaviour be kept separate from the investigator's interpretation of the behaviour which he has observed. When it is impossible to study all aspects of behaviour, the investigator must be selective in respect of the particular aspects of the total behaviour pattern which is to be observed and indicate these in his research design.
Time and incident sampling offer the advantage of allowing for patterns of behaviour to emerge under naturally occurring

conditions. They are useful methods to use to supplement information gained by the use of other research techniques, and they offer particular advantages for the study of individuals who may be unable or unwilling to respond to testing procedures or self-report techniques.

This form of data collection is very time consuming compared with other methods, and it should be confined to those aspects of behaviour which may not be evaluated by other means. If it is to be used as effectively as possible, however, the investigator ought to determine in advance whether time or incident sampling is to be employed; then observe and record enough of the situation to make the behaviour meaningful; record the incident as soon after the observation as possible; confine each report to a brief description of behaviour in a single specific situation; record the factual description of behaviour and the interpretation of it separately; carefully observe selected aspects of behaviour when these are prescribed in the research design; and collect a sufficient number of samples of behaviour before making inferences about typical behaviour.

THE CONTROLLED DIARY METHOD

If the individual is old enough and sufficiently intelligent, he may be requested to keep a diary in which he records certain aspects of his behaviour, e.g. his fear or anger responses. This technique has been made use of by Himmelweit *et al.* (1958) to study the television-viewing behaviour of children and more recently by Wragg (1968) to investigate the leisure activities of boys and girls.

The value of the results obtained in this way very much depends upon the character or the diarist. Whilst the diary may be kept for any period of time, there is an indication that the number of recordings progressively declines over a seven-day period (Anastasi 1948). This may occur because the individual's behaviour changes over the period of time, because it is influenced by the interest which is being taken in it by the investigator and by the individual himself. Alternatively it may be that the individual loses interest in the study and becomes less conscientious. For these reasons information gathered by means of the controlled diary method should be supplemented by information gathered by means of other research techniques.

RECORDING OBSERVATIONAL DATA

If observation is to be used as a method of collecting data for research purposes, objectivity is essential. Yet it is fairly well established that different descriptions of the same incident or event are given by different observers of the event (cf. Krech and Crutchfield 1948). This is partly due to their emotional involvement, their selective perceptions and their different powers of recall. In order to overcome the biases introduced by the human observer, various mechanical instruments have been made use of to obtain a more accurate record of events.

The use of cameras and tape recorders allows behaviour to be recorded and to be reproduced so that the nature of behaviour may be more accurately analysed. The use of other instruments, such as the stop watch, thermometer and dynamometer, allows behaviour to be measured to a degree of accuracy which could not be achieved by the human observer.

Many mechanical instruments have been constructed and are in wide use, but they are subject to certain limitations. They may be expensive and rather complex, and the research worker may be unable to afford to use them or may possess insufficient knowledge to use and maintain them. If they are used to study behaviour, their presence in the situation may affect the behaviour of the subject. For example, the presence of an undisguised microphone in a classroom may influence the behaviour of some if not all of the children. When used efficiently, however, they enable the observer to record behaviour accurately and objectively.

CHECK LISTS

Other techniques have been developed to overcome observer bias. These techniques are not mechanical in nature, but they serve to direct the observer's attention to relevant aspects of behaviour and to record the data obtained in a systematic manner.

A check list or a schedule is a simple device consisting of a prepared list of items which are thought by the research worker to be relevant to the problem being investigated. After the name of each item a space is provided for the observer to indicate the presence or absence of the item. This check list draws the attention of the investigator to relevant factors and enables him to record the data quickly yet systematically.

Check lists are sometimes used in the form of a questionnaire which is completed by the respondent rather than by the observer. They are most frequently used in this way to investigate opinions and attitudes. Reference should be made to Oppenheim (1966) for a more extensive discussion of the use of check lists for this purpose.

RATING SCALES

An observer may be asked to judge the behaviour he sees and to classify it into categories. This is essentially the task he performs when completing a schedule, but he can also be asked to give a numerical value or rating to his judgements. The use of ratings implies that some form of scale is being used on which behaviour is measured, but the measurement of behaviour in this way presents many problems to the social scientist because behaviour cannot usually be measured in standardized units that convey the same meaning to everyone. Social scientists, however, have developed a number of scaling techniques which enable them to ascribe numerical values or ratings to their judgements of behaviour.

To construct a rating scale the research worker identifies the variable to be measured, places categories or units on a scale to differentiate varying degrees of that factor and describes these units in some way. Whilst no rule governs the number of units that are used on a scale, having too few categories tends to produce crude measures that have little meaning, and having too many categories makes it difficult for the rater to discriminate between one unit and the next on the scale.

The scale units may be expressed in terms of points or numbers or one or two word phrases. These terms, however, do not always contain sufficiently precise information nor convey the same meaning to all people, and more specific phrases may be used to enable the rater to identify more clearly the characteristics to be rated.

Sometimes specimens of work are used to describe units on a scale. Essays or samples of handwriting that represent various levels of performance may be placed on a continuum by a judge or preferably by a panel of judges. The sample or specimen to be evaluated can then be compared with the specimens used in the scale. Burt suggested this approach as long ago as 1921 in the evaluation of essays, and Thorndike's handwriting scales have been in use since 1918. Some intelligence tests manuals also provide scaled specimens for determining the mental age of children as revealed by their drawings. The technique is also being used in the Certificate of Secondary Education procedure for the evaluation of essays.

The construction and use of a valid, reliable and objective rating scale poses a number of problems, the most important of which is that of clearly defining the factor which is to be evaluated and conveying this information to the raters. It is also important to realize that the effectiveness and the validity of a scale depends upon the characteristics of the raters. Some raters may possess limited information or insufficient knowledge to make judgements about the factor to be rated, but this may not prevent them from doing so. Others may rate factors differently, that is from a different frame of reference, especially if precise instructions have not been given them or if they are unaware of the precise purpose of the rating procedure. Many writers also draw attention to the influence of what has been called the 'halo' effect or the 'rater-ratee interaction error'. This is the tendency of the rater to be influenced with respect to one characteristic by his general or overall impression of the individual. This error can be reduced or eliminated by warning the rater of the possibility of its occurring, and by rating one characteristic or trait and discussing the rating before proceeding to the rating of the remainder. There is evidence, too, which suggests that there is a tendency for raters who are at one extreme on a personality trait either to rate others at the other extreme (rater-trait interaction error), or to rate others at the same extreme (similarity error). Finally attention has been drawn to the tendency of raters to be too generous or too severe, especially when the self-interests of the raters are threatened.

The interview

The interview technique is a widely used method of gathering data, for some people are more willing to provide information in a face-to-face situation, especially if the interviewer is skilled in establishing good relationships with the interviewees. The interview technique is frequently used for diagnostic and therapeutic purposes by psychiatrists, for educational and vocational guidance by psychologists and for personnel selection by employers and their staff. Here, however, we shall be mainly concerned with its use in research.

The great advantage of the interview as a method of gathering information lies in the flexibility of approach it permits. The interviewer is able to explain the purpose of the study and can ensure that the subject fully understands what is required of him. If the interviewee misunderstands a question the interviewer can add a clarifying remark, and can encourage him if he appears to lack interest or motivation. The interviewer can also acquire information on the respondent's behaviour which could not be obtained in any other way. His attitude towards the interview situation and his reaction to the questions may in certain circumstances be important for the purpose of the research. A further advantage is that the flexibility of the approach is particularly valuable when information is sought from children and illiterates, and from those who would possibly not be approachable in any other way, as, for example, in the case of emotionally disturbed adults and children.

The interview can be used in different ways for research purposes—the way in which it is used in any particular project depending upon the research worker, who must decide whether it enables him to gather the information he is seeking. Because of the richness of the data it provides, it may be used in the initial stages of a project in an effort to clarify the problem and to discover possible lines of research. It can also be used as the main method by which data is collected (see Belson 1967), or be used in conjunction with other techniques to supplement their findings, or even clarify them.

TYPES OF INTERVIEW

Interviews may be classified according to the purpose for which they are used and according to their design or structure.

Interviews are carried out for two different purposes: there are those which seek information which is factual in nature—what the subject 'knows'; and there are others which seek information on attitudes, opinions and beliefs—what the subject 'is'. In the former case the respondent is used to provide factual information which could be obtained in other ways, possibly through the use of a written questionnaire or by means of documentary analysis. In the latter case the respondent is asked to provide information which is entirely subjective, namely his attitudes and opinions.

STANDARDIZED INTERVIEWS

Interviews vary in design or structure—some are highly structured or standardized, others are unstructured or unstandardized. A standardized interview is one in which the procedure to be followed is determined in advance of the interview. The same questions are presented in the same manner and order to each subject, and the wording of the instructions to the subject is specified. The procedure must be strictly adhered to by the interviewer and he has no freedom to rephrase questions, add extra ones, or change the order in which they are presented. A number of research instruments may be used by the interviewer in the standardized interview situation, including tests, questionnaires, inventories and scales. These instruments must be administered in a standard way to all subjects—the administrator adhering strictly to the instructions prescribed in the manual.

Standardized interviews impose a degree of formality which does not permit the interviewer to establish the kind of relationship between himself and the interviewee which is necessary if the interview is to be conducted at any depth. On the other hand, the similarity of presentation introduces controls which allow generalizations to be made from the information which has been collected. The information gained from each respondent is comparable and errors due to differences in interviewer technique are minimized.

UNSTANDARDIZED INTERVIEWS

Unstandardized interviews are those in which the technique is more flexible. The series of questions to be asked and the procedure to be followed may be decided upon beforehand, but the interviewer is permitted to deviate from these if the situation appears to demand it. He can thus change the wording of the questions and the order in which they are presented, follow up unexpected clues, and even alter the direction of the inquiry. This form of approach is especially useful if the studies are to be carried out at some depth. However, the chief disadvantage of the unstructured approach is that the data gained in this way cannot be easily compared, and generalizations may not be possible.

The research worker must familiarize himself with the unstandardized and standardized interview techniques, for both types may be appropriately used in different research situations.

PREPARATION OF THE INTERVIEW

It is necessary to plan for the interview if it is to be effective in obtaining the information which is required in order to test the research hypothesis. The research worker must have a clear idea of the sort of information he needs, and he must prepare questions which will extract that information. A clearly defined procedure must be formulated which will include the instructions to the subject and the sequence in which the questions will be given.

The success of an interview very much depends upon the skill and sensitivity shown by the interviewer. The co-operation and confidence of the subject must be gained, and this is best done by creating a friendly and permissive atmosphere. An initial period spent talking to the subject about a topic of interest will often establish a situation in which he is willing to provide the information which is sought.

It is inevitable that subjects will individually react to the interviewer and that some will be influenced by his or her characteristics. Interviewers differ in sex, age, social background, dress, speech, colour of skin and in personality, and differences in these characteristics may influence the subjects' replies. This is particularly so with regard to interviews concerned with problems which are sensitive in character. Responses to questions relating to sexual matters, colour and religion will be particularly affected. However, the effects of some of the characteristics will be minimized if a good relationship is established with the subject.

As a result of experience in the use of interviews for research purposes, certain principles have been developed to guide the behaviour of the interviewer:

1. The interviewer must convey the impression to the subject that he is in possession of information or knowledge which the interviewer needs and which no one else can provide.
2. The respondent must be assured that the information given will be confidential.
3. If the interviewer is outside the hierarchical structure in which the subject works or studies, then the subject should be informed of this.
4. The interviewer must be pleasant and restrained in manner rather than too friendly. He should also avoid giving the impression of being superior, patronizing, clever or sly, and should not threaten or bully the subject.
5. The rules of the interview or the procedure to be followed must be carefully followed.
6. The interviewer should avoid giving hints by his facial expression or his tone of voice as to the answers he would prefer to be given.

If these principles are ignored, biases will occur in the data which is obtained. Some of these biases can be eliminated by the careful selection and training of interviewers, but others are inevitable and they must be taken into account when the data is interpreted.

RECORDING INTERVIEW DATA

The replies of respondents have to be recorded by some means. It is possible to do this by taking written notes of the responses during the interview, but this can affect the nature of the relationship between the interviewer and the subject, and can of course be extremely time consuming. However, it does have the advantage of being a complete and accurate record of the responses to which reference can be made after the interview, and it removes one source of bias in that what is recorded is not selected by the interviewer.

To overcome the disadvantages associated with note taking during the interview, some interviewers prefer to make notes after the interview has finished. This is an appropriate strategy to adopt in certain circumstances, but the obvious danger is that the interviewer may recall only a small proportion of the points made by the subject. It has been estimated that only 40 per cent of the important points raised in replies are recalled by even experienced interviewers, and this percentage would be insufficient for research purposes.

The use of a tape recorder is undoubtedly the most convenient way of recording the results of an interview. In this way the interviewer is freed from the necessity of writing out the subject's responses during the interview, and can concentrate upon making notes of aspects of the subject's behaviour which he observes. The tape recording provides a complete and accurate record of the entire interview. It also preserves the emotional and vocal character of the replies, and the errors that are sometimes made in written records are avoided.

INTERVIEWING CHILDREN

The interviewing of children presents rather special difficulties. One difficulty is that of determining the child's level of linguistic and conceptual development in order to phrase questions which are meaningful to him. A good deal of research is being undertaken (see Wallace 1965) in an attempt to determine the ages at which children develop an understanding of various kinds of concepts, and reference must be made to some of the findings by those seeking to interview children.

Children can respond verbally from the age of two years, but initially their response is imitative rather than self-generated. Some items in tests of intelligence designed for use with young children require the child to name objects or to repeat one or two word phrases, and are based upon the assumption that children of two and a half years of age are capable of making such a response.

Interviews which consist entirely of verbal material are unlikely to be successful with children below the age of eight years, since children often find difficulty in persisting in a verbal situation. For this reason interviews are often conducted in play situations using dolls and various types of apparatus in order to establish rapport and to maintain the child's interest. Many tests of intelligence, e.g. the Stanford-Binet and the WISC, contain items which involve the use of apparatus and allow for a non-verbal response—the child being required to manipulate the apparatus in making his reply. Some children, especially those who are overactive or withdrawn, may be distracted by the apparatus and their co-operation may be difficult to obtain. Such children, however, invariably present considerable difficulties to the interviewer, and even experienced interviewers are sometimes unable to establish contact with them or to elicit meaningful responses.

The interviewing of children demands a high level of skill from the interviewer; it has been described as an art. Many interviewers appear to be able to establish and maintain a relationship because of their manner and form of approach. It is essential that the child's co-operation be obtained; otherwise the responses will not be forthcoming. If a child is interviewed out of his home or classroom he may feel insecure. One of the interviewer's tasks in this case is to make the child feel secure, perhaps by allowing his parent to be present, although this is not always desirable. Once a feeling of security is achieved responses are more likely to be obtained.

Certain principles have been suggested for gaining the co-operation of children in an interview:

1. Interview the child in a situation with which he is familiar.
2. Allow a parent to be present if this is considered necessary.

3. Adopt a welcoming friendly attitude towards the child.
4. Use games and apparatus especially with young children.
5. Adopt a flexible, child-centred approach to the interview, if necessary following the child around the room and asking questions at appropriate moments. This demands a thorough knowledge of the questions to be asked.
6. Be prepared to be patient and persistent.

EVALUATION OF THE INTERVIEW

The chief advantage of the interview is the flexibility of approach it allows. Such flexibility, however, permits the introduction of a considerable degree of bias, in that interviewers may differ widely in approach and in appearance. Even the standardization of the procedure and the careful selection and training of interviewers does not rule out all sources of bias: differences will remain in the manner in which questions are asked by different interviewers and these differences may well influence the responses obtained.

Interviews are extremely expensive and time consuming, especially in comparison with methods which do not require the presence of an interviewer, for example, questionnaires sent through the post. Interviewers must be selected and trained and this can take time. They also require a salary or a fee and their expenses must be paid. Long periods of time may be spent with each interviewee, and unless a large number of interviewers are employed or subjects are interviewed in groups, any study which involves large numbers of subjects will take a long time to complete.

As has been said, the chief advantage of collecting information without the use of interviewers is the relative cheapness of the method. Fewer staff are required to administer the instruments used and to tabulate and analyse the results obtained. A large sample distributed over a wide geographical area can be studied comparatively cheaply and quickly. Since no interviewers are required, the possibility of interviewer bias is ruled out. There are, however, certain disadvantages in this approach. In the absence of an interviewer the technique used must be self-explanatory. The instructions must be unambiguous, and phrased with the least intelligent subject in mind. Even if these precautions are taken, it will still be the case that those subjects who are illiterate cannot be members of samples from whom data is to be collected. A further disadvantage is that bias may be introduced by the respondents who may not complete the technique, e.g. a questionnaire, in accordance with the instructions. A time lapse may occur between the reception of the questionnaire and its completion by the subject. During such a time lapse the subject may seek the advice of his friends, or may consult a literary source and thus introduce a source of bias for which the research worker may not have provided.

But perhaps the chief disadvantage in not using an interviewer is the very poor response rate to a technique, especially if it is sent through the post. It is possible, of course, to anticipate this and to counteract its effects by sending out techniques to a larger sample than is required for the purposes of the study, but this safeguard does not rule out the possibility of bias, because the group of subjects who return the technique is not usually representative of the original sample to whom it was sent. There is often a reason why some subjects fail to respond. This reason varies from study to study, and it is an important task of the research worker to determine the nature of the reason if this is possible.

CHAPTER 8

Some statistical concepts related to research

Earlier we briefly discussed the notions of test reliability and validity, test standardization, and regression to the mean. In this chapter a few more points are outlined which will enable the reader to have a better appreciation of some of the issues which arise in the design of experiments in education and in the analysis of their results, or in test construction. At the same time it is stressed that this is not a text on statistics or experimental design, and readers interested in studying these subjects further should consult appropriate books.* The treatment here is essentially elementary, but it is hoped that it will illuminate some problems that have been raised in earlier chapters and introduce one or two new issues. An understanding of the points discussed here will enable the reader to make a better judgement of the value of reported research.

Random sampling

The term *population* indicates any arbitrarily designated group, for example, all the ten-year-olds in Scotland. A *representative sample*, on the other hand, is one which reflects the characteristics of the parent population from which it was selected, in true population proportion, of course. Now normally one cannot know, thoroughly, the characteristics of the parent population and so we cannot hand-pick, as it were, the specific items which go to make a representative sample. In these circumstances the best way to select a *random sample* is by the use of random selection

* See, for example, LEWIS, D. G. (1967) *Statistical Methods in Education* and (1968) *Experimental Design in Education*. London: University of London Press Ltd.

procedures. Indeed, it is only by using samples chosen by such methods that we can employ inductive statistics and make inferences about the parent population on a probability basis.

Random sampling can be without, or with, replacement from a finite population. In the former a random sample is obtained if two conditions hold. First, the individuals in the population must have an equal probability of being selected on the first draw. Second, as individuals are selected, each remaining individual in the population must have an equal chance of being selected on the next draw, and so on. Thus if we wish to select, say, five persons out of a group of thirty, we place the thirty names in a hat, draw one out and keep it out. On the next draw we select another name. Clearly this procedure allows that each person in the population, or remaining in the population, has an equal probability of being selected.

But sampling can also be with replacement. In this approach the first name withdrawn from the hat is replaced and a second draw carried out from the thirty names again. It is, of course, possible for the same name to be selected on two or more occasions. But because it is not usually sensible to, say, test the same pupil twice, or interrogate the same person twice, sampling with replacement is rarely used in educational research. Put more formally, sampling with replacement from a finite population of size N, yields a random sample of size n, if in each draw each individual in the population has a probability of $1/N$ of being selected, while the draws are independent.

Using random sampling without replacement we can thus derive two or more random samples which can be used as experimental or control groups for the purposes of experimental research, as indicated in the last chapter. But there are also other modes of sampling such as *systematic* and *stratified sampling*, although these are more involved and will not be discussed here.*

* See BUTCHER, H. J. (1966) *Sampling in Educational Research.* Manchester: Manchester University Press.

Further, we can sample by schools rather than by individuals. The important point is for readers to note precisely how the sampling was made in a particular piece of reported experimental research, as this will help him to judge the likely value of the results.

Null hypothesis

One frequently meets the term *null hypothesis* in research literature. Its significance can be illustrated as follows.

Consider again some entire population such as all the ten-year-olds in Scotland. Any measure based on an entire population is called a *parameter* or 'true measure', whereas a measure based on a sample is called a *statistic*. Thus a mean which is a parameter would involve, in our instance, a mean based on data relating to all the ten-year-olds in Scotland. Now in many experiments our interest may not be within what limits the parameter may be confidently said to lie, as in the one possibility that the parameter is zero. For example, we may wish to know if the correlation between two sets of marks is zero, or if the difference between the means of two sets of marks differs from zero. In these instances we must test the hypothesis that the degree of correlation is zero, or that the difference in means is zero. Such hypotheses—that the parameter is zero—are known as *null hypotheses*. More formally it can be said that the null hypothesis states that no difference exists between a sample statistic and a hypothetical population value.

If a statistic is of such a size that the null hypothesis can be completely rejected, then it is said that the statistic is *significant*. For example, consider the case where two random samples of pupils are taught a new topic each by a different method. At the close of the experiment suppose that the difference in mean achievement (on a test equally fair to both groups) is greater than could reasonably be attributed to fluctuations in random sampling. In other words, the difference is of such a size that we must reject the null hypothesis at some level of probability and say that the difference is significant. Note carefully, however, that we have not necessarily found the cause of the difference. In rejecting the null hypothesis we have rejected the view that the difference in achievement between the groups was due to chance fluctuations in random sampling. Rejection of the null hypothesis does not, in itself, prove that the difference in mean achievement was due to difference in method, or to some other factor not properly controlled. Often, of course, it is entirely reasonable to suppose that the independent variable was the effective influence after the rejection of the null hypothesis.

Standard error

If we, say, weighed all the nine-year-old girls in Scotland and found the arithmetic mean of their weights, we should establish a parameter. Such a task would require much time and effort and would not normally be feasible. Accordingly we would take, say, 100 groups each containing 30 such girls and weigh these. Now the 100 means would vary somewhat. In fact they would cluster around the true mean (obtainable only if the whole population could be weighed) and, moreover, be normally distributed around it. While it is not possible to determine the true mean, or the extent of the divergence of the obtained mean of one sample from the true mean (or of several samples), we can assess the probable limits of the error by calculating what is known as the *standard error*. Stated in general terms, the standard error is the standard deviation of the sampling distribution, in our example the sampling distribution of means.

It will by now be appreciated that any measurement we make based on a random sample (i.e. on a statistic)—be it mean, standard deviation, correlation, etc., involving attainment, intelligence, height, weight or any other characteristic—is likely to be in error to a greater or lesser extent. Thus when any statistic is calculated such as correlation coefficient or difference in means, the standard error must also be calculated. The statistic is then compared with its standard error in order to see if a statistic of the given size could have been obtained by chance. This book is not the place to indicate how the standard error is calculated or how the comparison is made, as these are matters to be treated in books which deal specifically with statistics. But it is important for the reader to appreciate that if the research worker gives a statistic he must also make it clear if one of the obtained size could be attributed to random sampling. If it cannot be so explained, then the null hypothesis must be rejected at a given level of probability and the statistic recognized as significant.

Data in categories

So far we have been discussing issues relating to scores on a continuous variable such as school marks or scores on an achievement test. Sometimes, however, data can only be put into discrete categories, as when we divide pupils by sex, assess them on some trait in terms of A, B, C, D and E gradings, or indicate their performance as good, fair, poor and so on. In such cases the significance of group differences is studied by calculating a statistic known as *chi-squared* (χ^2). Here is a typical problem. We may wish to find out, for example, if

		Grades					
		A	B	C	D	E	*Total*
Numbers of	Boys	3	9	26	10	2	50
	Girls	1	5	22	17	5	50

there is a significant difference in the numbers of boys and girls getting various grades in physics, the cell numbers in the accompanying illustration indicating the number of children in each cell. The chi-squared test enables us to find the degree of divergence between the numbers actually obtaining the various grades, and the numbers that we would expect in the cells on a proportionate basis if there was no difference in the performance of the sexes. Tables of chi-squared will then indicate the probability that a value of chi-squared as large as that obtained could arise by chance. If, for example, a value as large as that found could arise on a chance basis less than 5 times in 100, we may feel free to reject the null hypothesis and accept that there is a difference in the numbers of boys and girls obtaining various grades in physics.

Levels of significance

It will be appreciated that the level of probability at which the null hypothesis is rejected is an arbitrary decision made by the research worker. The null hypothesis is often rejected in education if the size of a statistic is such that the probability of its arising by chance is less than 5 in 100. In other disciplines the figure may have to be less than 1 in 100 or 1 in 1,000 before a statistic is accepted as significant. The important point is that the reader should examine research reports to see at what level of probability the null hypothesis was rejected.

Item analysis

It is necessary to be aware of what is meant by the term *item analysis* and to have a general idea of how this is carried out. Item analysis indicates which items in an objective test are too easy or too difficult, and which may fail for other reasons to discriminate clearly between the better and poorer examinees. When reading research literature, it is necessary to watch carefully to see if item analysis has been carried out when certain kinds of tests have been constructed, for example, tests involving measured ability and attainment. A test whose items have been revised and finally selected on the basis of this procedure is certain to be more reliable than one made up of an equal number of unanalysed items. There are two aspects of the problem to be considered, item difficulty and item discrimination.

ITEM DIFFICULTY

The difficulty of a test item is numerically equal to the p per cent of the group which had the item correct, providing all subjects have had time to attempt all items. If sufficient time is not available, the position is a little more complicated. For most tests, roughly equal numbers of items with $p=95$–85 per cent, 84–75 per cent, , . . . , 14–5 per cent are selected, assuming that the test is to be used with children whose ability or attainment, as the case may be, spreads across the whole range. On the other hand, if we are concerned, say, with the top 40 per cent of subjects, then most of the test items should have p values close to $p=40$ per cent and the distribution of test scores need not be normal.

ITEM DISCRIMINATION

This index compares the passing or failing of a particular item with success on the test as a whole. In other words, it indicates the degree to which a test item detects individual differences in the characteristics which the test as a whole is required to measure.

There are a number of ways of calculating the index of item discrimination involving, say, biserial coefficient of correlation and tetrachoric coefficient of correlation. These methods depend upon a certain technical knowledge which will not be discussed here. A simple method, often adequate for some purposes, is as follows. Divide the test papers into a top group—roughly 27 per cent of the total group—comprising those who obtained the highest scores on the test, and a bottom group consisting of an equal number of papers with the lowest scores. The number of correct responses in the lower group is then subtracted from the number of correct responses in the upper group, and this difference is divided by the number of test papers in the top (or bottom) group. This quotient, expressed as a decimal fraction, is the *index of discrimination* (Johnson 1951).

Test items which have an index of discrimination equal to 0·40 or higher are generally regarded as good items. Those with indices between 0·30 and 0·39 need revising and improvement, while those with indices below 0·30 must be either radically revised or rejected. It should also be noted that indices of item discrimination are liable to have considerable sampling error,* regardless of the way in which they are calculated. An item which appears very disciminating in one small sample may not be so in another. The use of large samples obviously helps in this respect.

When reported research involves the construction and use of objective tests it is important to see that effective item analysis has been carried out.

* A sampling error is the difference between the value of some statistic (e.g. mean or standard deviation) obtained from a sample and the value which would have been obtained had it been calculated on the basis of the whole population.

CHAPTER 9

Examples of research in education

In this chapter examples are drawn from five broad areas of educational research. These examples illustrate:

A) The collection of data to be used as a basis for administrative action if so desired
B) Research relating to social and economic conditions affecting educational progress
C) The evaluation of educational progress
D) Experimental research
E) Research related to child development

All the examples are drawn from investigations which are nationally known.

It must be stressed that only brief descriptions of the researches are given here, and in fairness to those responsible for the projects readers should study the original references for themselves. The summaries give the briefest outlines of the research. Moreover, questions are posed from time to time about the investigations. *These questions are not intended to imply any criticism whatever of the studies; rather they are to encourage the reader to look carefully at research reports and even to give him some little experience in doing so.*

A) The collection of data to be used as a basis for adminstrative action can be a simple or a complex enterprise. The two examples given here are taken from part of appendix 14 of volume 2 of the Plowden Report. The first deals with the effects of the variations in the standard of provision of primary school education on both the numbers of pupils still at school at seventeen years of age and on the number of pupils entering higher education.

Data for both primary and secondary schools were collected for the year 1961–2 in respect of the following indices:

Expenditure on teachers' salaries, in pounds per pupil
Total cost per pupil in pounds per pupil
Expenditure debt charges (reflecting the debt incurred in building new schools since 1945)
Percentage of classes over-size (more than thirty pupils per class)
Number of teachers released for special advanced courses per 1,000 teachers

Table 1 (p. 618) shows that the standards of provision of primary education were distributed more unequally than most aspects of the standards of provision in secondary schools. In technical terms, the coefficient of variation (which is taken as one hundred times the standard deviation divided by the mean) of the above indices for primary schools was either equal to or greater than the coefficient of variation for the corresponding indices for secondary schools.

Some of the indices for measuring 'outputs' of secondary schools were:

a) Number of pupils aged 17 as a percentage of those at school four years earlier in 1962
b) Number of new awards to universities per 1,000 population aged 17–19 averaged for the years 1960–2
c) Full value LEA awards tenable 1961–2 at non-university institutions per 1,000 population; average of the three age groups 17, 18, 19 in 1961
d) Lesser value LEA awards tenable 1961–2 a tnon-university institutions per 1,000 population; average of three age groups 17, 18, 19 in 1961
e) Number of students entering teachers' training colleges per 1,000 population; average of three age groups 17, 18, 19 in 1961
f) Total number of new awards (university plus non-university)

and training college entrants per 1,000 population aged 17–19, averaged for 1960–2.

Table 2 (p. 618) shows the correlation coefficients, or the degrees of association between certain of the indices measuring the provision of primary school education and the indices measuring the 'outputs' of secondary schools. The expenditure on teachers' salaries per pupil in primary schools correlated with the indices of secondary school 'outputs' as follows: +0·32 with (a); +0·22 with (b); +0·22 with (c); +0·18 with (d); +0·16 with (e); and +0·27 with (f). In the case of the other indices of primary school provision, the correlations with indices of secondary school 'outputs' were either smaller or even negative. Generally, the equivalent indices of secondary school provision correlated more highly with the indices of 'output'. Moreover, the correlations between the indices of provision of primary school education and the corresponding ones for secondary school education were, on the average, higher than the correlations between the former indices and the indices measuring 'outputs'. The author of the appendix concluded:

i) The direct effect of the variation in standards of provision of primary education on secondary school 'outputs' is likely to be small.

ii) The pattern of the 'outputs' from each LEA would be unaffected by a slightly different pattern of variation in standards of primary school provision between LEAS.

This is a most interesting piece of work of its type. It is suggested that readers carefully examine the appendix and then ask themselves these questions:

1. From how many LEAS were the data collected?
2. What are the advantages and disadvantages in using the coefficient of variation (as calculated) as a measure of the degree of inequality of indices?

3. Is it possible to collect reliable data for all the indices in question?
4. Do the tables in the appendix provide data which make a sound basis for any or all of the deductions that the author has drawn?
5. In particular is it safe, from the data provided, to conclude that a small redistribution of funds available for primary education would give greater financial support to LEAs with bad social conditions without affecting the pattern of student 'outputs'?
6. Can you think of other indices to measure variations in educational provision which, in your view, would be more influential in affecting student 'output'?

In the second example the author deals with the variations in standards of primary school provision with certain other social conditions.* The indices used to measure the provision of primary school education were the ones used earlier, while new indices measuring certain aspects of social conditions were calculated. Examples of the latter are:

Males in administrative, managerial and professional occupations as a proportion of economically active males, 1961
Males in semi-skilled or unskilled occupations as a proportion of economically active males, 1961
Proportion of private households living at more than 1½ persons per room, 1961
Proportion of dwellings with one to three rooms, 1961
Population aged 5–11 years per 1,000, 1961

Table 3 (p. 621) shows the intercorrelation of indices of social conditions and confirms, as had been indicated by other workers, that a high proportion of children of primary school age, low

* Only part of the study is discussed here. Readers must study the appropriate appendix in the Plowden Report for the remaining details of the investigation.

value dwellings, overcrowding, poor housing amenities, low social class, etc., all show positive correlations with one another. Together these conditions create an environment which is disadvantageous to scholastic progress. Table 4 (p. 623) shows the correlation between the indices of standards of primary school provision and these social conditions. The intercorrelation coefficients are generally low, and there is less variation in the more important indices of standards of provision than in the indices of social conditions. In the author's view, the evidence taken as a whole suggests that a primary school system has been built which neither ensures positive discrimination in favour of, nor against, the culturally disadvantaged areas.

This is an example of a piece of research which produced facts on which action could be taken if the central government deemed it desirable to do so. It was, for example, open to the government to devote more money to give better educational facilities in the disadvantaged areas and thus show some positive discrimination in their favour. Readers may now like to ask themselves these questions:

1. In which areas of the country were the social conditions studied? How were the areas selected?
2. How were the data on the social conditions obtained?
3. Can such data on social conditions be objectively and reliably obtained?
4. What evidence from table 4 supports the author's contention that expenditure per pupil on debt charges (reflecting the proportion of school places built since 1945) tended to be lowest in deprived areas?
5. How strong is the evidence that the primary school system as of the time of the Plowden Report neither ensured positive discrimination for, nor against, culturally disadvantaged areas?

Although social conditions and educational provision may well change, and the data obtained in this research become completely out of date, the investigation will remain a useful one of its type.

B) We now turn to an example of research which relates social and economic conditions to actual progress. Details will be found in appendix 9 of volume 2 of the Plowden Report. In the opening sentence (p. 349) of his report of the Manchester survey, the author states that the aim of the inquiry was to investigate the relationship between the educational attainment of primary school children and environmental factors. Children aged 10 years in 1964 were studied, since they 'had received the full impact of primary school education'. Moreover, the actual pupils studied had taken certain standardized tests of reasoning and attainment at 7, 8, 9 and 10 years of age. Performance on these tests provided the criterion for school progress, although to be fair to the author it must be stressed that he was well aware of the limitations in using this as a criterion. Altogether about 2,000 ten-year-olds, drawn from forty-four schools out of a total of 176 primary schools in the Manchester area, provided the sample. Prior to the main experiment, a pilot study was carried out in three schools.

Three broad groups of variables, all thought likely to influence school progress, were used,* namely, home, neighbourhood and school variables. Under the first group came variables such as *cleanliness of home, parental occupation, percentage of children's families with criminal record.* In the second group came variables such as *play areas near home, number of incidents of breaking and entering school January* 1960–*spring* 1964, while under the last group of variables came *size of class, percentage attendance for junior department* 1962–3, and *turnover of teachers.* A full list of variables together with the basis and source of the assessments made in respect of the variables are given in annex 1 to appendix 9 and should be carefully studied.

* See also WISEMAN, S. (1964) *Education and Environment.* Manchester: Manchester University Press.

K

For each of the twelve tests of reasoning (I.Q.) and attainment, the percentages of pupils with a standard score <85 and >115 were calculated, as well as the average score for the school. Thus with twelve tests and three measures for each there were thirty-six criterion scores. Altogether there were eighty-seven variables which when intercorrelated (for the forty-four schools) yielded 3,741 correlation coefficients. On pp. 356–62 of the report there are a number of important tables reporting various correlations. For example, table 3 (p. 357) shows the average correlation of home, neighbourhood and school variables with the thirty-six test variables. Thus we find, say, that the cleanliness of the home correlates +0·475, and the percentage of children in the school receiving free meals −0·471, with the test variables.

The examination of correlation coefficients, while very important, is, as it were, a 'surface analysis'. It is also important to try to establish what underlying trends are discernible, and to do this the intercorrelation coefficients are subjected to what is termed a principal components analysis. In essence, a large number of correlations are replaced by a small number of components, dimensions or factors. Thus table 8 (p. 364) shows that the first component is correlated with school, neighbourhood and home variables; also it is responsible for by far the greater part of the variability of scores on the educational tests. Further, when this dimension is examined closely, it is seen that it is the home variables which are most affecting educational progress. Thus the author concludes (p. 365) that at the primary stage of education it is the adverse factors at work in the home which are the overwhelming ones, and that, because of the fewer and lower correlations between the school variables and dimension one, the school seems to be doing little to counteract the home influence. Moreover, in paragraph 57 (p. 365) the author stresses that within the important sector of the home, both the quality of the mother's care and poverty are closely connected with scholastic attainment.

After a careful study of the report in appendix 9 of volume 2 of the Plowden Report, readers may like to ask themselves the following questions:

1. Did those responsible for the survey appear to work from clear testable hypotheses, or did they start from the general assumption that there would be a relationship between home, school and environmental variables on the one hand, and school progress on the other. Or is the study an example of an *ex post facto* analysis of the problem?
2. Which of the variables in annex 1 to appendix 9 can be obtained objectively?
3. One of the variables assessed was *appearance and sociability* of the children. Do you consider it possible to give a global but interpretable five-point rating on general behaviour, appearance (no penalty for worn but clean clothing) and attitude to observer?
4. What are the views expressed in the report on the problem of whether or not the size of the correlations between environmental variables and attainment rises with age?
5. What reasons are given in the report for contending that little emphasis should be placed on the positive relationship found between streamed schools and test performance?
6. 'The limitations of correlational analysis are many, and it must be remembered that the figures we have presented here are measures of association: they are not (necessarily) indications of causality.' What does this statement mean?

The first part of the study was, as we have seen, a 'schools analysis' based on forty-four schools. The second part deals with data obtained from 186 pupils and their parents. These pupils were drawn from twenty-two schools and for them there were, of course, the results of the twelve tests of intelligence, English and arithmetic given at 7, 8, 9 and 10 years of age. There were also available for each child ratings on a number of home and school variables that had been used in the other study but which were applicable to individual pupils, e.g. cleanliness of home, neighbourhood crime. But other new 'family' variables were introduced.

Three analyses of the data were made. In one the actual scores obtained on the tests were used as criterion measures. For the second analysis the criterion measures were whether or not a child was backward (standard score <85) on each test, so a straight dichotomy backward: not backward was used as a simple scoring device for each of the intelligence and attainment measures. In the third analysis a bright (standard score >115): not bright dichotomy was used as a scoring device on each test.

Table 12 (p. 375) shows that in the case of the first analysis the first principal component or factor 1—the only significant factor—good scores on the tests tend to be obtained by those pupils who possess parents with a good attitude to education and who come from homes where both they themselves and their parents read books. In the 'brightness' analysis there was also one component or factor of significance. It showed that brightness was most closely associated with the variables of parents' preference for grammar school education for the child, parents' membership of the public library, and parents' and children's reading in the home.

After studying the report of the pupils' analysis readers will find it a useful exercise to ask themselves the following questions:

1. While it is true that the variables comprising literacy in the home and attitude to education have the highest correlations with test scores, these correlations are only modest in size. Why do you think this is so?
2. What evidence is there that environmental influences may have a greater adverse effect on the above average than on those pupils of average ability?
3. The pupils' analysis does not support the emphasis given to the factors of cleanliness and crime in the schools' analysis. What comment is made on this in the report?
4. How reliably could the variable 'husband's interest' be

assessed? Would your experience lead you to believe that the scale used for assessing 'books in house' was a useful one?

5. On what grounds does the author of the report conclude (p. 381) that the influences affecting backwardness tend to be those denoting the mother's care to the child, while for brightness the parents' attitude to education seems to be the most important?

C) Our third example of research deals with the evaluation of educational progress. Data have been taken from appendix 7 of volume 2 of the Plowden Report and concern the standards of reading of eleven-year-olds in the years 1948–64. It must be stressed that the data deal with the evaluation of the educational progress of groups and not of single individuals.

The test used to assess national standards in 1948, 1952, 1956, 1961 and 1964 was the Watts-Vernon Test. It examines reading comprehension by posing thirty-five questions which the child has to answer by selecting the correct reply from five given words —that is, it is a multiple-choice test. It takes ten minutes to administer. The range of difficulty is ample for junior school pupils, but it does not adequately extend the abler pupils in secondary school. Most readers will not have seen the test, but they can get a fair idea of its format by studying the NFER Sentence Reading Test 1, although they should bear in mind that the latter is for junior school children only.

The report points out (p. 263) that the early questions in the test seem to measure reading, the later ones comprehension. It then argues that since the test is used to assess group and not individual performance, the effects of particular test items which may be biased for or against an individual candidate are 'ironed out'; that is, good and bad fortune due to such items are randomized. Again, although the test shows a bias in favour of boys, this does not matter since it is constant and does not invalidate the comparison of scores made between one testing and the next. The report also considers the important issue of sampling, and discusses whether or not the samples of children tested were fair and accurate. It shows that the standard error of the mean score of pupils aged eleven years decreased between 1948 and 1964.

The results for 1948, 1952, 1956 and 1964 surveys are presented in table 1 (p. 261) and diagram 1 (p. 263),* the latter showing a plot of the percentile rank against the raw score. At all levels of reading ability there has been an improvement in score. For example, in 1948 the score at the tenth percentile was 3·9 and the score at the ninetieth percentile 18·5, the corresponding scores in 1964 being 7·5 and 22·8. It is concluded that in 1964 boys and girls of eleven reached, on the average, the standard of reading attained by pupils seventeen months older in 1948.

After studying the report readers may like to pose to themselves the following questions:

1. What does the report say about the fairness and accuracy of the sampling procedures used in these studies?
2. What does the report have to say about the possibility of a 'zero error' on this test? (A 'zero error' is the tendency for present candidates to obtain higher mean scores on tests standardized many years ago because of the increased sophistication of children in respect of psychological tests.) Do you consider that a 'zero error' is important when considering the results of these reading surveys?

D) It is difficult to give an example of experimental research in education which is nationally known. The one very briefly outlined here is that which involves the Initial Teaching Alphabet reading experiment, although it must be stated at the outset, and

* Fuller details can be obtained by studying: Ministry of Education (1956) *Standards in Reading*, 1948–56, and Department of Education and Science (1966a) *Progress in Reading*, 1948–64. London: H.M. Stationery Office.

in clear terms, that many criticisms have been made of the experimental design used and of the analysis of the results obtained. It is assumed that readers will know what is meant by i.t.a.

Downing (1964) has outlined the intended characteristics of the experimental design. It was his wish to compare the progress made in reading by at least 2,500 children starting school and commencing reading using i.t.a. with a matched control group starting reading with the traditional alphabet and spelling. In the experimental schools the dependent variable was the medium in which the beginning books were printed, with the teaching method and contents of the books used remaining the same as they had been previously. Local educational authorities which provided a varied cross-section of the school population were asked to allow schools to take part. After head-teachers had received a pamphlet outlining what it was hoped to do, and meetings with teachers held, schools were selected for the first phase of the experiment. Other schools were chosen to provide control classes using the traditional medium.

There were, in fact, to be two lines of control. First, each school was to be its own control in the sense that the results of attainment in reading and other subjects for the experimental classes were to be compared with results from the school's control classes of children who were using readers printed in traditional orthography. Second, there was a sample from a matched control group where only traditional orthography was used.

For the teachers in the experimental classes there were training workshops. Further, parents were helped to use i.t.a. materials so that they could support the teachers, since parents of children using the traditional alphabet also aid teachers in respect of reading. Moreover, the teachers in the control schools were provided with refresher courses and they attended meetings to discuss research in reading. By these means it was hoped to equalize for 'enthusiasm' in respect of the teaching of reading. The first phase of the experiment began with children entering school in September

1961, and the second phase with those entering in September 1962.

Downing also stresses that many criteria were used to measure the effects of i.t.a. Both the experimental and control groups underwent regular testing in respect of the mechanics of reading and reading comprehension. More than that, account was taken of such factors as attitudes to books, creative writing ability, and general linguistic, intellectual and emotional development. Further, the testing programme had not only to consider the progress made in the early stages of using i.t.a., but also to evaluate progress in the later stages after a transition had been made to traditional orthography and spelling.

As already stated, many criticisms have been made of the design of the experiment and of the analysis of the results. It is not our intention to be critical in this way, but readers are invited to find for themselves the answers to the questions given below by studying, say, Southgate (1965) or Downing (1967) where many of the voiced cautions and criticisms can be found.

1. Precisely how were the schools, and the experimental and control classes selected within the chosen LEA areas?
2. Were the children in the classes representative samples of the chosen population?
3. Was the stimulus provided for the teachers using traditional orthography equal to that provided for teachers using i.t.a. as their medium?
4. To what extent do you consider that the results obtained from the experiment were due to the new alphabet *per se*?
5. Did some children appear to benefit more from i.t.a. than others? If so, who were these pupils?

E) In conclusion we say a few brief words about Piaget's theory of intellectual growth as an example of a theory derived from observation and experiment, and from an interpretation of his findings made from within a conceptual framework. His real interest was in genetic epistemology* and he used the growth of intelligence as a bridge between his early interest in biology and his somewhat later interest in epistemology. Put more formally, we may say that he was primarily interested in the theoretical and experimental investigation of the qualitative development of intellectual structures.

In some of his studies Piaget merely observed children, and their behaviour was not in any way elicited by him. But in most of his investigations there is evidence of the formal properties of experimentation proper in the sense that the behaviour was elicited by some stimulus provided by the experimenter. It is, however, important to stress that his work was often carried out with very small and unrepresentative samples of children. But against this it must be realized that the number of experiments he carried out in many diverse fields was very large. When analysing his observations or the results of his contrived experiments he did, of course, make certain assumptions. In other words, he started from 'a point of view' when interpreting his data. One assumption was that if the term 'logic' is taken in the broad sense to mean a set of actions that obey logic-like rules, then it can be said that at all age levels behaviour and thought manifest some form of logic. In the infant, the logic seen in its behaviour is more primitive and less systematized than that of the pre-school or primary school child, while it is only in adolescence that a formal logical system of thought is elaborated comparable to that used by logicians.

So Piaget provided a theory of intellectual growth which suggests that the child goes through a series of stages of intellectual growth which are qualitatively different from one another. Moreover, the intellectual structures which define earlier stages

* Epistemology is the theory or science of the method or ground of knowledge.

are integrated into those of the stages that follow. Thus the order of stages is invariant.

Piaget's theory of intellectual growth is the most useful one that we have at present, especially for teachers. It can give great help in facilitating our understanding of why it is that children have such difficulties with certain concepts. Moreover, his order of stages has been found to be invariant in all experiments in all cultures studied to date. Nevertheless, it is, at times, quite inadequate to explain all the facts, and one day it will be subsumed under, or replaced by, a more all-embracing one. Indeed, we can conclude by heartily agreeing with Sir Cyril Burt—an early and distinguished worker in the field of educational research—that science is essentially progressive, with each new theory making an advance on the last but which, in itself, is never final.

Further reading

BORG, W. R. (1965) *Educational Research: An Introduction.* London: Longmans.

BUTCHER, H. J. (ed.) (1968) *Educational Research in Britain.* London: University of London Press Ltd.

DAVIES, J. T. (1965) *The Scientific Approach.* New York: Academic Press.

FOWLER, W. S. (1962) *The Development of Scientific Method.* London: Pergamon.

FREEDMAN, P. (1960) *The Principles of Scientific Research.* London: Pergamon.

GOOD, C. V. (1963) *Introduction to Educational Research* (2nd edition). New York: Appleton-Century-Crofts.

HIGSON, C. W. J. (1968) 'Finding out about educational research.' *Educ. Res.*, **11**, 31–7.

MACINTOSH, H. G. and MORRISON, R. B. (1969) *Objective Testing.* London: University of London Press Ltd.

MEDAWER, P. B. (1969) *Induction and Intuition in Scientific Thought.* London: Methuen.

PIDGEON, D. A. and YATES, A. (1969) *An Introduction to Educational Measurement.* London: Routledge and Kegan Paul.

TRAVERS, R. M. W. (1964) *An Introduction to Educational Research.* London: Collier McMillan.

VAN DALEN, D. B. (1966) *Understanding Educational Research.* London: McGraw-Hill.

Bibliography

ANASTASI, A. (1948) 'A methodological note on the "controlled diary" technique.' *J. genet. Psychol.*, **3**, 237–41.

ANSTEY, E. (1966) *Psychological Tests*. London: Nelson.

BELSON, W. A. (1967) *The Impact of Television: Methods and Findings in Program Research*. London: Crosby Lockwood.

BERG, I. S. (1961) 'A case study of developmental auditory imperception.' *J. Child Psychol. Psychiat.*, **2**, 86–93.

BEVERIDGE, W. I. B. (1957) *The Art of Scientific Investigation*. London: Heinemann.

BIGGS, J. B. (1962) *Anxiety, Motivation and Primary School Mathematics*. London: Newnes.

British Psychological Society (1966) *Psychological Tests: A Statement*. London: British Psychological Society.

BROWN, C. W. and GESELLI, E. E. (1955) *Scientific Method in Psychology*. New York: McGraw-Hill.

BUROS, O. K. (ed.) (1965) *The Sixth Mental Measurements Yearbook*. New Jersey: Gryphon Press.

BURT, C. (1968) 'Brain and consciousness.' *Br. J. Psychol.*, **59**, 55–69.

BUTCHER, H. J. (1966) *Sampling in Educational Research*. Manchester: Manchester University Press.

CATTELL, R. B. (1957) *The Sixteen Personality Factor Questionnaire* (Revised edition). Champaign: Institute for Personality and Ability Testing.

CATTELL, R. B. and BELOFF, H. (1962) *High School Personality Questionnaire*. Champaign: Institute for Personality and Ability Testing.

CHAZAN, M. (1964) 'The incidence and nature of maladjustment among children in schools for the educationally subnormal.' *Br. J. educ. Psychol.*, **34**, 292–304.

CRONBACH, L. J. (1960) *Essentials of Psychological Testing*. New York: Harper.

Department of Education and Science (1966a) *Progress in Reading, 1948–64*. London: H.M. Stationery Office.

Department of Education and Science (1966b) *Statistics in Education*. London: H.M. Stationery Office (published annually).

DEWEY, J. (1933) *How We Think*. Boston: D. C. Heath.

DOUGLAS, J. W. B., ROSS, J. M. and COOPER, J. E. (1967) 'The relationship between handedness, attainment and adjustment in a national sample of school children.' *Educ. Res.*, **9**, 223–32.

DOWNING, J. A. (1964) *The i.t.a. Reading Experiment*. London: Evans.

DOWNING, J. A. (ed.) (1967) *The i.t.a. Symposium*. London: NFER.

DREVER, J. (1956) *A Dictionary of Psychology*. Harmondsworth, Middlesex: Penguin Books.

EDWARDS, A. L. (1957) *Techniques of Attitude Scale Construction*. New York: Appleton-Century-Crofts.

EVANS, K. M. (1965) *Attitudes and Interests in Education*. London: Routledge and Kegan Paul.

EYSENCK, H. J. and EYSENCK, S. B. G. (1963) *Eysenck Personality Inventory*. London: University of London Press Ltd.

EYSENCK, S. B. G. (1965) *Junior Eysenck Personality Inventory*. London: University of London Press Ltd.

GARDNER, D. E. M. (1950) *Long Term Results of Infant School Methods*. London: Methuen.

GESELL, A. (1955) *The First Five Years of Life*. London: Methuen.

GUILFORD, J. P. (1959) *Personality*. London: McGraw-Hill.

GUILFORD, J. P. (1967) *The Nature of Human Intelligence*. London: McGraw-Hill.

HARRIS, C. W. (ed.) (1960) *Encyclopedia of Educational Research* (3rd edition, p. 1160). New York: Macmillan.

HIMMELWEIT, H. T., OPPENHEIM, A. N. and VINCE, P. (1958) *Television and the Child*. London: Oxford University Press.

JACKSON, L. (1957) *A Test of Family Attitudes*. London: Methuen.

JOHNSON, A. (1951) 'Notes on a suggested index of item validity: the U-L index.' *J. educ. Psychol.*, **62**, 499–504.

JOHNSON, M. E. B. (1966) 'Teachers' attitudes to educational research.' *Educ. Res.*, **9**, 74–9.

KING, W. H. (1965) 'Differences in mathematical achievement related to types of secondary schools and their geographical locations.' *Educ. Res.*, **8**, 74–80.

KRECH, D. and CRUTCHFIELD, R. S. (1948) *Theory and Problems of Social Psychology*. New York: McGraw-Hill.

LAWSON, K. S. and HARTLEY, C. J. (1967) 'The vocational aspirations of educationally subnormal children.' *Occup. Psychol.*, **41**, 223–9.

LEWIS, D.G. (1967) *Statistical Methods in Education*. London: University of London Press Ltd.

LEWIS, D. G. (1968) *Experimental Design in Education*. London: University of London Press Ltd.

LIKERT, R. (1932) 'A technique for the measurement of attitudes.' *Archs. Psychol.*, **22**, no. 140.

LINDZEY, G. and BORGATTA, E. F. (1959) 'Sociometric measurement.' In LINDZEY, G. (ed.) *Handbook of Social Psychology*. London: Addison Wesley.

LOVELL, K. (1967) *Educational Psychology and Children* (9th edition). London: University of London Press Ltd.

MCASHAN, H. H. (1963) *Elements of Educational Research*. New York: McGraw-Hill.

Ministry of Education (1956) *Standards in Reading*, 1948–56. London: H.M. Stationery Office.

MORENO, J. L. (1953) *Who Shall Survive?* New York: Beacon House.

MORRISON, A. (1967) 'Attitudes of children towards international affairs.' *Educ. Res.*, **9**, 197–202.

National Foundation for Educational Research (1968a) *Twenty-second Annual Report*. Slough: NFER.

National Foundation for Educational Research (1968b) *Educational Guidance in Schools*. Slough: NFER.

National Foundation for Educational Research (1969) *Test Agency Catalogue*. Slough: NFER.

NORTHWAY, M. L. and WELD, L. (1957) *Sociometric Testing: A Guide for Teachers*. Toronto: University of Toronto Press.

OPPENHEIM, A. N. (1966) *Questionnaire Design and Attitude Measurement*. London: Heinemann.

PEEL, E. A. (1948) 'Assessment of interests in practical topics.' *Br. J. educ. Psychol.*, **17**, 41–7.

PIAGET, J. (1968) 'Explanation in psychology and psychophysiological parallelism.' In FRAISSE, P. and PIAGET, J. (eds) *Experimental Psychology: its Scope and Method*–1. London: Routledge and Kegan Paul.

PIDGEON, D. A. (1965) 'Date of birth and scholastic performance.' *Educ. Res.*, **8**, 3–7.

Plowden Committee (1967) *Children and Their Primary Schools.* London: H.M. Stationery Office.

POPPER, K. R. (1959) *Logic of Scientific Discovery.* London: Hutchinson.

RAVEN, J. C. (1951) *Controlled Projection for Children.* London: Lewis.

SHAW, M. E. and WRIGHT, J. M. (1967) *Scales for the Measurement of Attitudes.* New York: McGraw-Hill.

SOUTHGATE, V. (1965) 'Approaching i.t.a. results with caution.' *Educ. Res.*, **7**, 83–96.

STOTT, D. H. (1961) 'An empirical approach to motivation based upon the behaviour of a young child.' *J. Child Psychol. Psychiat.*, **2**, 97–117.

STRONG, E. K. (1943) *Vocational Interests of Men and Women.* Stanford: University of Stanford Press.

TAYLOR, P. H. (1966) 'The role and function of educational research—3.' *Educ. Res.*, **9**, 11–15.

TERMAN, L. M. and MERRILL, M. A. (1937) *Measuring Intelligence.* Boston: Houghton Mifflin.

TERMAN, L. M. and MERRILL, M. A. (1959) *Measuring Intelligence.* Boston: Houghton Mifflin.

TERMAN, L. M. and ODEN, M. H. (1959) *Genetic Studies of Genius: The Gifted Group at Mid-Life.* London: Oxford University Press.

THACKRAY, D. V. (1965) 'The relationship between reading readiness and reading progress.' *Br. J. educ. Psychol.*, **35**, 252–4.

THOMPSON, G. (1961) *The Inspiration of Science.* London: Oxford University Press.

THURSTONE, L. L. and CHAVE, E. J. (1929) *The Measurement of Attitudes.* Chicago: University of Chicago Press.

VERNON, P. E. (1956) *The Measurement of Abilities* (2nd edition). London: University of London Press Ltd.

VERNON, P. E. (1968) 'What is potential ability?' *Bull. Br. psychol. Soc.*, **21**, 211–19.

WALLACE, J. G. (1965) *Concept Growth and the Education of the Child.* Slough: NFER.

WECHSLER, D. (1949) *Wechsler Intelligence Scale for Children.* New York: Psychological Corporation.

WISEMAN, S. (1964) *Education and Environment.* Manchester: Manchester University Press.

WISEMAN, S. and FITZPATRICK, T. F. (1955) *Devon Interest Test.* London: Oliver and Boyd.

WRAGG, M. (1968) 'The leisure activities of boys and girls.' *Educ. Res.*, **10**, 139–45.

YATES, A. and BARR, F. (1960) 'Selection for secondary technical courses: a report of a pilot investigation.' *Educ. Res.*, **2**, 143–8.

Index

Anastasi, A., 111, 148
Anstey, E., 74, 148
attitude scales, 103 ff.
  equal-appearing intervals scale, 104–5
  summated ratings, 105

Bacon, F., 2, 6
Belson, W. A., 116, 148
Berg, I. S., 43, 148
Beveridge, W. I. B., 2, 148
Biggs, J. B., 32, 148
Borg, W. R., 147
British Psychological Society, 71, 148
Brown, C. W. and Geselli, E. E., 54, 148
Buros, O. K., 81, 83, 148
Burt, C., 146, 148
Butcher, H. J., 125, 147, 148

case study, 40–4
  advantages and limitations of, 43–4
  biographical type, 42–3
  clinical type, 41–2
Cattell, R. B., 101, 148
Cattell, R. B. and Beloff, H., 101, 148
Chazan, M., 36, 148
check lists, 113
construct, 19–20
controlled diary method, 111–12
Cronbach, L. J., 71, 81, 100, 148

data in categories, 128–9
Davies, J. T., 147
Department of Education and Science, 35, 142, 148, 149
descriptive research,
  procedures, 29–34
  types of, 34–47
developmental studies, 44–7
  cross-sectional approach, 45
  longitudinal approach, 45–7
Dewey, J., 8, 149
Douglas, J. W. B., Ross, J. M. and Cooper, J. E., 38, 149
Downing, J. A., 144, 149
Drever, J., 85, 149

educational research,
  aims of, 24–5
  examples of, 132 ff.
  some points to watch in, 26–7
  types of, 22–4
Edwards, A. L., 105, 149
Evans, K. M., 105, 149
experimental and control groups, 55–6
experimental controls, 53–4
experimental designs, simple, 57 ff.
experimental research,
  stages in, 49–51
Eysenck, H. J. and Eysenck, S. B. G., 101, 149
Eysenck, S. B. G., 101, 149

Fowler, W. S., 147
Freedman, P., 147

Gardner, D. E. M., 109, 149
Gesell, A., 33, 43, 149
Good, C. V., 147
Guilford, J. P., 20, 149

Harris, C. W., 22, 149
Higson, C. W. J., 147
Himmelweit, H. T., Oppenheim, A. N. and Vince, P., 111, 149
hypothesis testing, 52

incident sampling method, 110–11
instruments of research, 64 ff., 85 ff., 108 ff.
  evaluation of, 64–5
  introduction, 64–71
  reliability, 68–71
  validity, 65–8
interview, the, 115 ff.
  children, 120–2
  evaluation, 122–3
  preparation, 118–19
  recording data, 119–20
  standardized, 117
  types of, 116
  unstandardized, 117–18
inventories, 99 ff.
item analysis, 129–31

Jackson, L., 103, 149
Johnson, M. E. B., 32, 131, 149

King, W. H., 36, 149
Krech, D. and Crutchfield, R. S., 112, 150

Lawson, K. S. and Hartley, C. J., 36, 150
levels of significance, 129
Lewis, D. G., 62, 124, 150
Likert, R., 105, 150
Lindzey, G. and Borgatta, E. F., 107, 150
Lovell, K., 79, 150

McAshan, H. H., 22, 150
Macintosh, H. G. and Morrison, R. B., 146
matching techniques, 56–7
Medawar, P. B., 147
methods of acquiring knowledge, 1 ff.
Ministry of Education, 150
model, 19–20
Moreno, J. L., 106, 150
Morrison, A., 32, 150

natural and social sciences, differences in, 14–16
National Foundation for Educational Research, 32, 74, 78, 150
Northway, M. L. and Weld, L., 106, 150
null hypothesis, 126–7

observational techniques, 108 ff.
  direct methods, 108–9
Oppenheim, A. N., 98, 105, 113, 150

Peel, E. A., 100, 150
Piaget, J., 12, 145–6, 150
Pidgeon, D. A., 38, 147, 151
Plowden Report, 35, 38, 132 ff., 151
Popper, K. R., 18, 151
projective techniques, 102 ff.

questionnaires, 85–99
  administration, 95
  design, 91–3
  group, 97
  oral, 97
  postal, 95–7
  preparation of, 89–91
  questions, 93–5
  scope of, 89
  types, 86–9
  value of, 97–9

random sampling, 124–6
rating scales, 113–15
Raven, J. C., 103, 151
reliability, 68 ff.
  coefficient, 70–1
  equivalent forms, 69–70
  split-half, 70
  test–retest, 69
research,
  aims of, 11–13
  descriptive, 29 ff.
  experimental, 49 ff.
  in education, 21 ff.
  role in theory in, 16–18
  types of, 20–1
reasoning,
  deductive, 4–5
  hypothetico-deductive, 8–9
  inductive, 6–7
regression to the mean, 62–3

self-report techniques, 85 ff.
Shaw, M. E. and Wright, J. M., 104–51
sociometric techniques, 106 ff.
Southgate, V., 144, 151
standard error, 127–8
Stott, D. H., 43, 151
Strong, E. K., 101, 151
surveys, 34–40
  advantages and limitations of, 40
  data sought in, 36
  level of complexity of, 37–8
  steps in the construction of, 38–9

Taylor, P. H., 25, 151
Terman, L. M. and Merrill, M. A., 70, 151
Terman, L. M. and Oden, M. H., 45, 151
tests, 71 ff.
  administration, 74–5
  aptitude, 82–3
  attainment, 83–4
  construction, 73–4
  group, 75–6
  individual, 76
  mental ability, 77 ff.
  non-verbal, 79
  pencil-and-paper, 76–7
  performance, 77
  types of, 75 ff.
  verbal, 79–80
Thackray, D. V., 38, 151
Thomson, G., 10, 151
Thurstone, L. L. and Chave, E. J., 104, 151
time sampling method, 109
Travers, R. M. W., 147

validity, 65 ff.
  coefficient, 68
  concurrent, 66–7
  construct, 67–8
  content, 65–6
  predictive, 66
Van Dalen, D. B., 147
variables, dependent and independent, 53
Vernon, P. E., 78, 80, 82, 151

Wallace, J. G., 120, 151
Wechsler, D., 81, 151
Wiseman, S., 137, 152
Wiseman, S. and Fitzpatrick, T. F., 100, 152
Wragg, M., 111, 152

Yates, A. and Barr, F., 101, 152